I AM NOT A
BASEBALL BOZO

HONORING GOOD PLAYERS WHO PLAYED
ON TERRIBLE TEAMS (1920-1999)

CHRIS WILLIAMS

Chris Williams

2021

SUNBURY PRESS

Mechanicsburg, PA USA

Published by Sunbury Press, Inc.
Mechanicsburg, PA USA

www.sunburypress.com

For information about special discounts for bulk purchases, please contact Sunbury Press Orders Dept. at (855) 338-8359 or orders@sunburypress.com.

To request one of our authors for speaking engagements or book signings, please contact Sunbury Press Publicity Dept. at publicity@sunburypress.com.

FIRST SUNBURY PRESS EDITION: October 2021

Set in Adobe Garamond | Interior design by Crystal Devine | Cover by Lawrence Knorr | Edited by Lawrence Knorr.

Publisher's Cataloging-in-Publication Data
Names: Williams, Chris, author.
Title: I am not a baseball bozo : honoring good players who played on terrible teams (1920-1999) / Chris Williams.
Description: First trade paperback edition. | Mechanicsburg, PA : Sunbury Press, 2021.
Summary : *I Am Not a Baseball Bozo: Honoring Good Players Who Played on Terrible Teams (1920–1999)* is a compendium of the best players on the worst major league teams of all time. Here's a stat-driven, humorous look at some of the brightest diamonds in the rough in baseball history.
Identifiers: ISBN : 978-1-62006-865-6 (softcover).
Subjects: SPORTS & RECREATION / Baseball / General | SPORTS & RECREATION / Baseball / History | HUMOR / Topic / Sports.

Product of the United States of America
0 1 1 2 3 5 8 13 21 34 55

Continue the Enlightenment!

Dedicated to my wife, Sue, who has lovingly and patiently put up with a bit of a baseball bozo for a long time.

Contents

Foreword

INBB. ThIose letters may not mean anything—until you have read Chris Williams' fascinating book. Then you will know the letters stand for: "I Am Not a Baseball Bozo"!

In other words: "I am not an incompetent player—a 'Baseball Bozo,' even though I was on one of the worst teams in baseball between 1920-1999."

Williams intriguingly focuses on good players on terrible teams. It's about time! We can all scroll through and remember players—who were fine players—but were saddled being on one of the worst teams in their league in a particular season. They may have been a "diamond in the rough"—but their baseball diamond team was very "rough," indeed! Their teams were awful! But these were competent players who had a "good year," statistically, even while their team was mired in the lower regions of the league.

William's approach is statistical. He outlines the criteria he used for identifying these players from the terrible teams. This assures his judgments are not based on his own baseball proclivities or favorites. The players were good; their stats prove it. Not that Williams is a fan of contemporary "sabermetrics" No way! Sabermetrics may have its place. But Williams writes: "The 'old' way of looking at the numbers is often looked-down-upon and subtly deemed to be relatively useless. This is an opinion I do not share, and I'm certain that there many baseball fans who agree with me." Instead, Williams says, "I will be using simple stats from a bygone era, numbers that often tell an accurate story that even the casual fan can understand and hopefully appreciate." We do appreciate these "simple stats"! But through it all and to put it all in perspective, Williams tells us: "Baseball is a game, not a religion, and when discussing it, I like to have a little fun." And this book is fun!

Each decade from the 1920s to 1999 gets a chapter. Williams interestingly sets the contexts by providing a list for each decade: "Some Important Stuff That Happened in the . . ." and "Some Important Things That

Happened in Major League Baseball in the..." These are great introductions to set the stage for the INBBs that come next.

For each year of the decade some of the "good players" on lousy teams for the year are mentioned. Williams describes their statistics and what qualifies each player to be able to win an "I am not a Baseball Bozo" award! This shows us ways the players' accomplishments were significant—when compared to the very bad teams on which they played.

Along the way there are those who deserve "Honorable Mention" for their stats—not quite good enough to win the coveted INBB award—but boasting better stats than their other more hapless teammates. Throughout, we get introduced to a wide group of players over these decades—names we may already know . . . and many we may not know!

Interspersed too are some "Sort-of Random Trivia" features. These are highly interesting . . . and entertaining. For example: "Hall-of-Fame pitcher Nolan Ryan broke into the majors with the Mets in 1966. Early in his career, his fingers would develop blisters after hurling five innings or so. To combat this, Ryan would soak his digits in pickle brine. As time went on, his fingers toughened up and he stopped the practice. From then on, opposing batters were in a "pickle" having to face Ryan's blazing fastball for a full nine." Who knew . . . ?!

Along our way in the remarkable journey Chris Williams provides, intriguing tidbits to warm the hearts of baseball fans:

Casey Stengel won a INBB award from Williams for his 1924 season. Like other fans, "Yankee star Mickey Mantle was somewhat amazed to learn that the 'Old Perfessor' was once a major leaguer. 'Sure, I played,' Stengel told his centerfielder, 'did you think I was born age 70 sitting in a dugout trying to manage guys like you?'" Classic Casey!

Williams' humor shines through in his "Honorable Mention" for 1985 to Jeff Leonard of the San Francisco Giants: "The outfielder cracked 17 home runs, drove in 62, and swiped 11 bases in 1985. A middling .241 batting average and terrible .272 OBP does keep the guy nicknamed 'Old Penitentiary Face' from winning an INBB outright. Honorable Mention." Then: "I wonder why they called him 'Old Penitentiary Face.' I've seen photos of the man. Doesn't look like a crook to me. Just sayin' . . ."

Did you know that Ivy Andrews, a 1932 INBB "winner" as a pitcher with the Boston Red Sox had the nickname: "Poison"? Williams says, "I was a little confused at first but now I think I get it . . ."

One of my favorite baseball trivia treasures turns up when Williams notes that the two men who wrote "Take Me Out to the Ball Game" (1908)—Jack Norworth and Albert Von Tilze—had never actually seen a professional baseball game before they wrote the song!

More directly about the game, we learn that "when Roger Maris slammed a then-record-breaking 61 home runs in 1961, he drew zero (0) intentional walks." Williams adds: "The fact that slugger Mickey Mantle (54 home runs himself) batted next in the batting order might have helped a little."

Also: "In need of a catcher, the 1962 Mets acquired Harry Chiti from the Indians for a player to be named later. After 43 plate appearances and a .195 BA, the Mets figured they already had enough under-performers (on a team that would eventually lose 120 games) and sent Chiti back to the Tribe as that player to be named later."

Williams' most engaging book is full of great information like this, introducing us to those players who were "gems" on their diamond teams even when their teams were far from polished! Along the way we pick up neat pleasures of baseball history—players, teams, and stories—giving us more than a "little fun" along the way! Through it all, Williams—the self-appointed "committee of one" to give out the INBB awards—invites us: "With a #2 Pencil or pen with black or blue ink, or crayon, write your choice 'INBB' or 'Honorable Mention'"!

What an entertaining book! This is pleasurable and enjoyable . . . full of all kinds of cool stuff! Thanks for introducing us to INBB and for writing this stat-filled and witty book, Chris Williams!

Donald K. McKim
Baseball Historian, Researcher, and Review Editor for Baseball
Almanac (www.baseball-almanac.com)

Acknowledgments

Thank you to Graphic Designer Nicole Williams for her fine work on the award icons. I would also like to thank the editorial staff at Sunbury Press for their diligent efforts in pulling this project together.

Introduction

I love baseball history. I especially have a warm place in my heart for play-ers who played on the bad teams of yesteryear. I think it's because I was a Phillies fan during my youth in the late 1960s and early 1970s. The team was abysmal but did have a few good players such as Dick Allen, Tim McCarver, Steve Carlton, Deron Johnson, and Rick Wise. Following those productive guys kept me following the Phils, otherwise, I might have abandoned that sorry bunch.

Fans of woebegone teams have little to root for as the losses pile up, and the post-season is an impossible dream. However, just like my childhood Phillies, many of these teams have some players who were like genuine diamonds in a sea of zirconium fakes. Rather than allow the pitiful cir-cumstances to blunt their competitive edge, these hardy diamond warriors perform well despite being surrounded by under/or non-productive roster mates. The accomplishments of these players are what many lousy team loyalists focus on to get them through the summer: "My team might be in last place, but our clean-up hitter has a good chance to drive in 100 runs." "What do you know? Our ace has a chance to win 20 games even though we're 88 games out of first." "Gee, this young kid just up from the minors has a chance to hit 20 home runs in only half-a-season."

I'm sure you get the idea.

In the chapters that follow, we'll discuss the recipients of the new "I Am Not a Baseball Bozo" (INBB) Awards. These productive guys, who played for the absolute worst teams from 1920–1999, are finally getting a little recognition. The criteria for qualifying for a coveted INBB are as follows:

1. An honoree must have played on a team that lost 100 or more games in a season. More-than-a-few bad clubs lost 90 or more games during the era, but the award is for guys who played for the worst-of-the-worst.

2. Position players need to have played in at least 2/3 of their team's games. From 1920 to1960, when both leagues played 154

games, award contenders needed to have appeared in at least 103 contests. In 1961, the American League expanded by adding two clubs, and the season increased to 162 games per team. To compensate for more contests, Junior Circuit INBB awards went to players who appeared in 109 games or more from 1961 on.

    In the National League, expansion didn't occur until 1962, so eligible players played in at least 103 games in 1960 and 1961. The standard increased to 109 games in 1962 and beyond.

3. For the period 1920-1960, to qualify for an INBB, starting pitchers must have compiled at least 142 innings and relief pitchers 48 innings. Beginning in 1961, the benchmark for AL starters rises to 150 innings and relievers 50 innings. The NL followed suit in 1962, with both leagues being judged by identical pitching standards for the rest of the decade.

4. The player must have performed at a level noticeably higher, statistically, than his teammates during the year considered.

5. More than one player from a team and year may win an "INBB" award.

6. A player may win more than once.

7. Winners will receive two vigorous virtual "thumbs-ups" and an enthusiastic cybernetic pat on the back from the Committee (which includes Baseball experts Mr. Me, Mr. Myself, and Mr. I). In addition, the Committee will cover all taxes.

8. In addition to the INBB, semi-productive guys who fell just below award criteria will be given an "Honorable Mention" along with a prize of a single robust pat on the back, tax-free.

SPOILER ALERT: This book contains a lot of baseball stats. It is numbers-driven; if you're looking for light, breezy, and analysis-free diamond stories, you are going to be very disappointed. Those that venture past this introduction will be, among other things, greeted with lots of statistics. Hopefully, not too many but be forewarned.

    For those of you who are into highly technical treatises complete with multitudinous statistical examinations of virtually every variable, you're going to be disenchanted, too. The "philosophical" underpinnings of this book can best be summed up with a quote from one of my previous baseball tomes:

Part of the enjoyment of following Major League Baseball comes from the examination of the statistics compiled by those who play the game. In the past, this was a lot easier to do as the basic stats were relatively few and simple to follow. In the 21st century, however, the number of categories created by the sabermetrics community seems endless. Using computer research, these highly intelligent folk have aided greatly in our understanding of the game. However, the "old" way of looking at the numbers is often looked down upon and subtly deemed to be relatively useless. This is an opinion I do not share, and I'm certain that there many baseball fans who agree with me.

I will be using simple stats from a bygone era, numbers that often tell an accurate story that even the casual fan can understand and hopefully appreciate.

In addition, diehard baseball traditionalists that view the game with reverent devotion might be offended by the pervasive air of goofiness and silliness. Baseball is a game, not a religion, and when discussing it, I like to have a little fun.

Got it?

Let's proceed!

Chris Williams
October 2021

ABBREVIATIONS

AB = at-bats

H = hits

HR = home runs

RBI = runs batted-in

W = walks

SB = stolen bases

OBP = on base percentage

SLG = slugging average

2B = doubles

3B = triples

E = errors

PCT = percentage

W = wins

L = losses

ERA = earned run average

WHIP = walks and hits per innings pitched

SV = saves

CHAPTER 1

The 1920s

You Ain't Heard Nothing Yet!

Some important stuff that happened in the 1920s:

- The 19th Amendment to the U.S. Constitution gave women the right to vote in 1920.

- On November 2, 1920, KDKA, Pittsburgh, became what many believe to be the first broadcast radio station to go on the air.

- The 18th Amendment mandated a ban on the sale, manufacture, production, and use of alcohol in the United States. The era of "prohibition" lasted until 1933.

- The tomb of ancient Egyptian ruler Tutankhamun is discovered in 1922, paving the way for comedian Steve Martin's hit comedy song, "King Tut."

- In 1925, future German dictator Adolph Hitler's manifesto of his twisted Nazi philosophy, *Mein Kampf*, is published.

- Aviator Charles Lindbergh became the first person to fly across the Atlantic Ocean. The flight from New York City to Paris took 33 ½ hours.

- A new era of entertainment dawned in February 1927 when the first motion picture with sound, *The Jazz Singer* starring Al Jolson, premiered in New York City.

- The New York Stock Exchange crashed, sending America and the world into "The Great Depression." The date: Friday, October 29, 1929.

Some important stuff that happened in Major League Baseball in the 1920s:

- 1920 is the year the Red Sox made the infamous sale of slugging pitcher Babe Ruth to the Yankees for 100,000 dollars (Back then, that was *a lot* of loot).

- A pitched baseball took the life of Cleveland Indians shortstop Ray Chapman in August 1920.

- Second baseman Rogers Hornsby captured the 1924 National League batting title with a blistering .424 AVG.

- The Kansas City Monarchs toppled the Hilldale Club to capture the first Negro League World Series in October 1924.

- In May 1925, Lou Gehrig replaced Wally Pipp as Yankee first baseman, beginning an incredible streak of 2,130 consecutive games.

- After an investigation, Commissioner Landis cleared stars Ty Cobb and Tris Speaker in January 1927 from accusations that they were involved in fixing a game in 1919.

- During the 1927 season, Yankee outfielder Babe Ruth hit a then-record 60 home runs.

- On December 1, 1929, the National League proposed a rule change calling for a "designated hitter" to bat in place of the pitcher. The American League rejected the plan.

- Here are the INBB award selections for the decade that has come to be known as the "Roaring Twenties." For teams like the Athletics, Phillies, and the Braves, things weren't quite so roaring; it was more like a death rattle . . .

◆ ◆ ◆

1920 Joe Dugan *(Philadelphia A's 48-106)*. Connie Mack liked to sign boys who had played college baseball to wear the A's uniform. Mack believed that a highly educated man was more than likely be more refined than the rough-and-tumble ruffians that dotted rosters all over the AL. No rowdy boys at Shibe Park, no siree. Infielder Joe Dugan, who went to Holy Cross, did well in 1920 (.322 AVG, .351 OBP, 40 doubles, 60 RBI). The college ranks did supply the dignified Mack with an abundance of potential candidates, but this practice often didn't translate into victories. Many of these collegiate prospects turned out to be crummy major league baseball players.

1920 Tilly Walker *(Philadelphia A's)*. Finished 3rd in the league in home runs with 17 and knocked in 82 teammates. Walker's OBP was passable (.321). Not great with the glove, he committed 22 errors over 149 games, but those power numbers carry him over the INBB line.

1920 Eddie Rommel *(Philadelphia A's)*. One of the first pitchers to use the knuckleball regularly, Rommel was a 22-year-old rookie in 1920. The man from Baltimore, Maryland, logged 174 innings as a starter and reliever, putting up a 2.84 ERA and 1.193 WHIP. He was later an umpire in the AL for 22 years.

1920 Dave Keefe *(Philadelphia A's)*. Another rookie that acquitted himself quite well for the White Elephants. Keefe earned an INBB for a 2.97 ERA and 1.220 WHIP. Keefe was never as effective in the majors, playing another four years, and finished with a career ERA of 4.15. His ball-playing days continued for another ten years as a minor league hurler, and he was later was hired to throw batting practice for the A's.

1920 Walt Kinney *(Philadelphia A's)*. Only appearing in ten games, Kinney gets two thumbs-up and a hearty virtual pat-on-the-back for a 3.10 ERA and five complete games over eight starts. He also made a couple of relief appearances.

1921 Cy Williams *(Philadelphia Phillies)*. One of the top sluggers in the NL, Williams finished with a .320 AVG and 18 HR. His .497 slugging percentage was 2nd best in the league. Williams (and the rest of the team) undoubtedly benefited from the hitter-friendly confines of Baker Bowl. How friendly? The right-field wall was a mere 280 feet from home and right-center only 300 feet away. The centerfield dimensions were closer to typical ballpark dimensions at 408 feet, but left field was an inviting 341 feet from the plate. Tons of home runs, doubles, and triples were hit at Baker Bowl over the years.

At Baker Bowl, the lefty-swinging Williams batted .325 and stroked 15 home runs. On the road, his HR production fell to 3, but he still hit .316 with ample RBIs. His overall performance deserves an INBB.

1921 Russ Wrightstone *(Philadelphia Phillies)*. A sort-of-prestigious Honorable Mention goes to the Phils' second sacker. His overall.296 AVG and 51 RBI are decent, but he only hit .237 on the road.

Before moving on, I should mention that a few Phillies compiled impressive stats in 1921 but did not appear in the required number of games (103) to qualify for an INBB. For example, Irish Meusel sizzled with a .353 AVG but only played in 84 games. Had he played in more games, he might have continued his hitting, but then again, he may have tailed off significantly. The same rationale applies to others who amassed good numbers but were used part-time.

Thanks largely to having played half of their games in the Baker Bowl, the pitching staff was a disaster statistically. No one even remotely qualifies for an INBB or Honorable Mention.

1921 Cy Perkins *(Philadelphia A's 53-100)*. Connie Mack's #1 backstop hit .288, smacked 12 HR, 31 doubles, and drove in 73 runs.

1921 Jimmy Dykes *(Philadelphia A's)*. The early 1920s were not kind to both Philadelphia baseball teams. The A's would rebound by the middle of the decade and by 1930 were an outstanding club. Jimmy Dykes would be an important part of those great squads. In 1921, a young Dykes blossomed with 16 homers, 32 doubles, 16 triples, and 77 runs batted in.

1921 Tilly Walker *(Philadelphia A's)*. Not much of a glove, leading AL left fielders in errors (22), Walker more than made up for it by having a great season at the plate. His line: .304 AVG, .389 OBP, 23 HR, 101 RBI, and .504 SLG.

1921 Frank Welch *(Philadelphia A's)*. One of the problems the A's had in 1921 was difficulty making the plays in the field they needed to make. Welch was a so-so centerfielder, making 12 errors, the 2nd highest amount of miscues in the league. A lively .285 average and satisfactory .347 OBP secured the man an INBB. He also led the A's in steals with six.

1921 Whitey Witt *(Philadelphia A's)*. Unlike neighboring Baker Bowl, Shibe Park's dimensions favored pitchers. Since it was decidedly harder to compile good hitting stats at 21st and Lehigh, Witt's totals look awfully good (.315 AVG, .390 OBP, 31 doubles, 11 triples.)

1921 Eddie Rommel *(Philadelphia A's)*. Rommel secures an INBB with16 wins, 3.94 ERA, 1.398 WHIP, and 20 complete games. On the verge of becoming one of the best pitchers in the league, Rommel would stick around long enough to become an important part of manager Mack's final round of pennant winners (1929-1931).

Sort of Random Trivia: Do you know what a "can of corn" is? No, I'm not talking about something you buy at the grocery store—I mean a baseball "can of corn." (Sorry. I didn't mean to insult your intelligence. I forgot I know that you know, and everyone reading this book almost assuredly knows that it is an easy fly ball.) The phrase has its' origin in an era when grocery store workers used their aprons to catch cans knocked off the top of a shelf. Cool beans, huh? Aren't you glad I shared that with you? Now you can amaze friends and families with that little factoid!

1922 Walter Holke *(Boston Braves)*. A top-notch fielding first baseman (.997), Holke hit a good .291, but it was an empty .291. Because he managed only 13 extra-base hits out of a total of 115 safeties and a low .317 OBP, Walter earned an Honorable Mention.

1922 Larry Kopf *(Boston Braves)*. Kopf's .266 BA and .332 OBP earn him an Honorable Mention. Like teammate Holke, a lack of extra-base power prevented Kopf from winning the soon-to-be-legendary "I Am Not A Baseball Bozo" Award. The veteran infielder began his major league career in 1913 and would retire after the 1923 campaign.

1922 Tony Boeckel *(Boston Braves)*. One of Hall-of-Fame pitcher Christy Matthewson's best friends, Boeckel, hit .289, logged a .349 OBP, and led the club in steals with ten. A productive six-year career was tragically cut short when Boeckel was killed in an automobile accident two years later. He was 31.

1922 Walton Cruise *(Boston Braves)*. With 104 games played, Walton slipped just over the amount required (103) to qualify for an INBB. Is (or was) "Walton" a common first name? I've never seen it before.

Wow, I think that's a neato handle.

Nonetheless, Cruise didn't allow the mounting losses to discourage him to the point that it negatively affected his performance in 1922. He was made of sterner stuff and soldiered on to give his team a .278 AVG, .360 OBP, and ten triples.

1922 Ray Powell *(Boston Braves)*. The Committee bestowed an INBB to Powell for a .296 AVG, .369 OBP, 11 triples, and 22 doubles.

1922 Frank Miller and Tim McNamara *(Boston Braves)*. Two hurlers manager Fred Mitchell could count on were Miller and McNamara. The 36-year-old Miller won 11 games, registered a decent ERA and WHIP numbers (3.51, 1.365), and completed 14 games.

The rookie McNamara didn't disappoint with a 2.42 ERA and 1.146 WHIP over 71 innings.

1923 Butch Henline *(Philadelphia Phillies 50-104)*. An INBB for the young catcher (.324 AVG, .407 OBP). Not only did he hit well at Baker Bowl, he racked up a .321 AVG and .376 OBP on the road.

1923 Walt Holke *(Philadelphia Phillies)*. Purchased by the Phils during the off-season, he batted .311 overall and hit 31 doubles. Holke hit a scorching .354 at Baker Bowl but a less impressive .270 on the road. Even though his home ballpark was a hitter's paradise, he still managed that .354 AVG against major league pitching, which not many others accomplished.

1923 Cotton Tierney *(Philadelphia Phillies)*. James Arthur Tierney from Kansas City, Kansas posted a .317 AVG and .352 OBP; he did better in road games with a .320 batting mark. A good but not great fielder, he had the 2nd best fielding percentage in the NL for second basemen. It was an INBB worthy season.

1923 Johnny Moken *(Philadelphia Phillies)*. Another guy who performed better away from the ridiculously comfy confines of Baker Bowl (.323 AVG, .412 OBP road, .303 AVG, .391 OBP home).

1923 Cliff Lee *(Philadelphia Phillies)*. I know I'm probably beating this to death, but there was a major difference between his stats at home and on the road. His overall average was competent (.317), but he only managed .270 away from home. Honorable Mention.

1923 Jimmy Ring *(Philadelphia Phillies)*. It would be easy to blame Baker Bowl for the team's astronomically high collective ERA of 5.34. However, the staff's ERA in road contests was a putrid 4.58. The fact is almost all of Philly's hurlers turned in bozo-like seasons; they sucked home *and* away.

Jimmy Ring was an exception. He managed a winning record (18-16) and 3.87 ERA and completed 23 games—an emphatic two-thumbs up and virtual pat-on-the-back for the 6'1", 170-pound right-hander.

1923 Stuffy McInnis *(Boston Braves 54-100)*. Once part of the A's famous "100,000 Dollar" infield, McInnis was traded away after asking for a salary increase that Connie Mack said he couldn't afford. After spending some time on the Red Sox and Indians, Stuffy was snatched off the waiver wire by the Braves. The smooth-fielding first baseman didn't disappoint with a .315 AVG and 95 RBI.

1923 Billy Southworth *(Boston Braves)*. As a manager, Southworth was one of the all-time best, capturing four pennants and guiding his clubs to a total of 340 games over .500. For his work as a skipper, the Veterans Committee selected him to the Hall of Fame in 2008. Southworth was a first-class player as well, finishing with a lifetime batting average of .297. For his accomplishments in 1923 (.319 AVG, .383 OBP, 16 triples, 78 RBI), the Braves' right fielder picked up an INBB.

1923 Rube Marquard *(Boston Braves)*. It was the veteran Marquard's last decent season (11 wins, 3.73 ERA, 1.381 WHIP). The Braves' staff wasn't horrible, so his numbers don't stand out in bold contrast. Even so, Ole' Rube deserves an INBB.

1923 Joe Genewich *(Boston Braves)*. A thinking, 21st-century baseball fan might ask, "Who the heck was Joe Genewich?" I even thought that myself. But after a little research, I discovered that the fellow pitched well-enough to last nine years in the majors, followed by a couple more seasons in the minors. All this scholarly effort resulted in an INBB for his work in 1923 (13 wins, 3.72 ERA, 1.399 WHIP).

1923 Jesse Barnes *(Boston Braves)*. Earlier in his career, Barnes was considered one of the best hurlers in baseball. After he registered a 6.25 ERA over the first two months of the 1923 season, Giants' manager John McGraw thought the 30-year-old veteran's best years were behind him and traded him to the Braves. Although Barnes didn't return to the form that saw him enjoy two twenty-win seasons, he did alright in Boston. Ten wins in a little more than half-a-season, a 2.76 ERA, 1.265 WHIP, and five shutouts are the stuff INBB Awards are made for.

1923 Johnny Cooney *(Boston Braves)*. A talented guy who put up a 3.31 ERA and 1.163 WHIP in 98 innings as a pitcher. Manager Fred Mitchell also used Cooney on a limited basis in the outfield and at first base. In 66 at-bats, Cooney batted .379 with a .414 OBP.

1924 Stuffy McInnis *(1924 Boston Braves 53-100)*. His offensive production fell noticeably but still wasn't bad (.291 AVG, 59 RBI). Stuffy's OBP was an abysmal .311, but he was nearly flawless at first with a .994 fielding percentage in 146 games played. Preventing hits and not committing errors that often lead to runs scored against is as important as producing runs for your club. McInnis deserves an INBB instead of just an Honorable Mention.

1924 Casey Stengel *(Boston Braves)*. A lot of baseball fans are surprised to learn that legendary manager Casey Stengel was also a ball player in his younger days and a good one at that. Yankee star Mickey Mantle was somewhat amazed to learn that the "Old Perfessor" was once a major leaguer.

"Sure, I played," Stengel told his centerfielder, "did you think I was born age 70 sitting in a dugout trying to manage guys like you?"

In 1924, Casey played 131 games and logged a .280 AVG and .348 OBP. In addition, he finished second among NL right fielders with a .977 percentage and was 4th in assists with 11.

1924 Bill Cunningham *(Boston Braves)*. Cunningham's major league career was brief, four years, and 1924 was his last season in the big show

(.272 AVG, .326 OBP, 13 steals to lead the team). Those numbers are good enough to earn him an Honorable Mention.

Cunningham also spent 12 years in the minors. A lot of the minor league teams at the time were independent and quite good. Many rosters were filled with talented players who were good enough to play in the majors but decided to play in cities like Amarillo, Sacramento, and Des Moines for often higher salaries, a chance to play every day, or a preference to live in smaller cities.

1924 Jesse Barnes *(Boston Braves)*. Even though Barnes led the league in losses (20), the rest of his numbers pass muster for an INBB (15 wins, 3.23 ERA, 1.289 WHIP, four shutouts, 21 complete games).

What does the phrase "pass muster" mean? I think it has something to do with successful military inspections. To be sure, I guess I could look it up, but I'm not in the mood.

I hope you understand.

1924 Johnny Cooney *(Boston Braves)*. Another good season for Cooney and another INBB (8 wins, 3.18 earned-run-average, and 1.249 WHIP). Once again, he put in a few innings at first and the outfield and batted a not-too-bad .254.

1925 Phil Todt *(Boston Red Sox 47-105)*. The Red Sox have had many good seasons over the decades, fielding some of baseball's greatest teams. However, the 1925 squad was one of the all-time worst. First baseman Phil Todt was one of a handful of guys on the roster who put up respectable stats (.278 AVG, .343 OBP, 11 HR, 13 triples, 75 RBI). He was also excellent in the field with a .991 percentage. INBB.

1925 Doc Protho *(Boston Red Sox)*. His only season with the Red Sox and the only year he was a full-time player, Protho delivered a .313 AVG, 51 RBI, and led the team in steals with nine. His .390 OBP was higher than the Fenway Parkers' winning percentage (.309). Later managed a bad Phillies team for three campaigns. Their lack of success was not his fault as he was a knowledgeable baseball man and a good field manager. The Phils had *major* financial troubles at the time.

"Every time we came up with a good player," Protho said, "we had to sell him in order to stay in business. It was a nightmare."

1925 Ike Boone *(Boston Red Sox)*. With a lifetime average of .321, the man proved he could hit. But Boone's eight-year career was interrupted twice by trips to the minors because of fielding troubles. His career fielding percentage was a bad .960, committing a whopping average of 21 errors per season patrolling right field at Fenway Park.

Despite a poor glove, skilled bat work in 1925 (.330 AVG, .406 OBP) merits an INBB.

1925 Ira Flagstead *(Boston Red Sox)*. He was no "Baseball Bozo" with a .280 AVG, .356 OBP, 61 RBI, and 84 runs scored.

Way to go, Ira!

1925 Tex Vache *(Boston Red Sox)*. He began his pro career at the age of 31, and 1925 was his only season in major leagues. In 110 games, Vache hit .313 with a .382 on-base-percentage. He might have lasted longer in the bigs, but he was an atrocious outfielder with a .908 fielding mark. Although the INBB Committee likes players with .300 and higher batting averages, they decided to give Tex just an Honorable Mention because of his fielding deficiencies. It's true; they cut teammate Ike Boone some slack despite *his* defensive shortcomings but as bad as he was, Vache was a lot worse.

1926 Topper Rigney *(Boston Red Sox 46-107)*. Red Sox fans during the latter half of the 1920s needed constitutions of iron to stay loyal to their favorite team. They were epically bad, but one of the team's starting infielders gave them a few things to cheer about. Topper Rigney was an excellent fielder, leading AL shortstops in fielding percentage and assists. Offensively, Rigney "only" batted .270 but walked 108 times, getting on base at a .395 clip. He also stroked 32 doubles and drove in 50 for a club that only scored 561 runs. Topper was "tops" and a solid INBB honoree.

1926 Jack Russell *(Boston Red Sox)*. The 20-year-old rookie showed his underachieving mound mates how it's done. His record was 0-5, but over 98 innings pitched, his ERA was 3.58 and WHIP 1.204. The staff ERA was a dismal 4.72 and collective WHIP a grim 1.517.

After his playing days, Russell settled in Clearwater, FL, and became a noted community leader. It was Russell who spearheaded the movement to get a baseball stadium built in the city. "Jack Russell Stadium" was later used by the Philadelphia Phillies during Spring Training from 1955-2003.

1927 Cy Williams *(Philadelphia Phillies 51-103)*. Williams was the NL home run champ with 30 dingers, 94 RBI, and .502 slugging. Even adjusting for the "help" he received from Baker Bowl, he had a good year with 15 HR and 42 RBI on the road.

1927 Fresco Thompson and Dick Spalding *(Philadelphia Phillies)*. Pardon me for grouping these two fellas; my thoughts about them are nearly identical (both-of-them hit better on the road than at home). INBBs.

> Fresco Thompson (.303 AVG, .343 OBP home; .308 AVG, .347 OBP road).
> Dick Spaulding (.296 AVG, .352 OBP home; .318 AVG, .377 OBP road).

1927 Jimmie Wilson, Heinie Sand, Russ Wrightstone, and Freddy Leach *(Philadelphia Phillies)*. The opposite reasoning applies to these four; their stats on the road were significantly lower than those they achieved at Baker Bowl. In-spite-of-this, they had decent years overall and deserved Honorable Mentions.

> Jimmie Wilson (.275 AVG, .330 OBP home; .260 AVG, .299 OBP road).
> Heine Sand (.299 AVG, .365 OBP home; .250 AVG, .320 OBP road).
> Russ Wrightstone (.306 AVG, .365 OBP home; .287 AVG, .342 OBP road).
> Freddy Leach (.306 AVG, .342 OBP home, .269 AVG, .316 OBP road)

1927 Dutch Ulrich *(Philadelphia Phillies)*. A native of Austria, Ulrich posted the 7th lowest ERA in the NL (3.17) and completed 14 games. A 1.247 WHIP cinched an INBB.

1927 Clarence Mitchell *(Philadelphia Phillies)*. The only other hurler on the Phils to put in numbers a major league pitcher wouldn't be ashamed of. His ERA was a little high (4.04), but his WHIP was OK (1.342), plus Clarence had the only winning record on the staff (6-3). Honorable Mention.

1927 Ira Flagstead *(Boston Red Sox 51-103)*. As a young man, Flagstead worked in a foundry, swinging a sledgehammer. As a result of all that hard work, Flagstead became a muscular stud. He was attracted to the sport of boxing and decided to try a career as a pugilist. That phase of his life lasted exactly one bout (a 15-rounder that ended in a draw) before deciding to make a full commitment to a sport that he loved and was quite good at, baseball.

Like all INBB Award winners, Ira endured a disastrous Red Sox season and thrived. The 33-year-old outfielder hit .285, registered a .374 on-base percentage, slugged 26 doubles and eight triples, and led the club in stolen bases with 12. With the glove, Flagstead owned the highest fielding percentage of any AL center fielder (.986) and was 4th in the league in assists (19).

1927 Jack Tobin *(Boston Red Sox)*. Tobin wrapped up his 13-year major league career in style with a .310 AVG and .371 OBP. Over 419 plate appearances, he fanned only nine times.

1927 Buddy Meyer *(Boston Red Sox)*. The Committee likes his .288 AVG, .359 OBP, and 11 triples but not the 40 errors he committed as an infielder (.939 percentage). Honorable Mention.

1928 Don Hurst *(Philadelphia Phillies 43-109)*. Acquired from the Cardinals in May, the rookie Hurst stepped right into the starting first base job. Along with a .285 AVG and .391 OBP, he sliced 19 home runs and plated 68 teammates. He also hit better overall on the road (.293 AVG, .401 OBP) than at the hitter's paradise Baker Bowl (.278 AVG, .371 OBP).

Have you ever heard anyone use the word "sliced" as a verb to describe home runs? I'm not sure it's appropriate; I'm pretty sure it's a Golf term. But I like the way it sounds.

1928 Fresco Thompson *(Philadelphia Phillies)*. Unlike 1927, Thompson did considerably worse on the road with the bat (.316 home, .260 road).

Even with this, the Committee decided to bestow an Honorable Mention for him, hitting 34 doubles, 11 triples, and stealing more bases than anyone else on the Phillies (19).

"Fresco" was Thompson's middle name; his real first name was "Lafeyette."

1928 Pinky Whitney *(Philadelphia Phillies)*. This was a tough one. Although Whitney hit 42 points higher at home (.322/.280), he also drove in 106 runs (46 on the road) which is hard to ignore. He also smacked as many circuit clouts away from Baker Bowl (5) as he did at home (5). Philly's rookie third sacker secures one of dem dar INBBs.

1928 Freddy Leach *(Philadelphia Phillies)*. The 30-year-old outfielder's line (.304 AVG, 13 HR, 36 2B, 11 triples, and 96 RBI). Leach also had a rifle arm, recording 29 assists. There's so much good stuff there that, well, Freddy deserved an INBB!

Deserved it, I tell you!

1929 No one lost 100 or more games, so no INBBs or Honorable Mentions were awarded.

The friendly confines of Baker Bowl helped inflate batting stats for the home team Phillies.

Cy Williams was one of the most-feared sluggers in the National League in the 1920s.

A stature of iconic A's manager Connie Mack. (Courtesy *Philadelphia Bulletin*)

Seasoned veteran Stuffy McInnis was a nice waiver pick-up for the 1923 Braves. (Courtesy Library of Congress)

Before a long career as a manager, Casey Stengel was a darn good baseball player (Library of Congress).

Jack Tobin's .310 BA gave Red Sox fans something to cheer about in 1927. (Courtesy Library of Congress)

A good pitcher AND hitter, Johnny Cooney earns INBB awards for 1923 and 1924. (Courtesy *The Sporting News*)

Cinema was changed forever when this flick introduced sound in 1927. (Courtesy Warner Bros.)

In 1924, the Kansas City Monarchs defeated the Hilldale club in the first Negro World Series. (Courtesy Library of Congress)

The 1930s

Prosperity is Just Around the Corner

Some important stuff that happened in the 1930s:

- The Empire State Building in New York City opened on May 1, 1931. At 1,454 feet, it was the tallest skyscraper in the USA until the World Trade Center twin towers opened in 1970.

- On May 22, 1932, Amelia Earhart became the first woman to fly alone in an airplane over the Atlantic Ocean.

- In November 1932, Franklin D. Roosevelt is elected President of the United States. He will eventually be elected three more times.

- Nazi party leader Adolph Hitler rose to power as Germany's Chancellor in 1933. A systematic persecution of Jews and other minorities began culminating with "The Final Solution" and the deaths of at least six million people.

- Beer, wine, and alcoholic spirits flowed freely again in America when the 21st Amendment was enacted, ending Prohibition. December 5, 1933.

- "The Labor Day Hurricane of 1935" struck the Florida Keys as a Category 5 storm and resulted in the deaths of 408 and millions of dollars in property damage.

- In August 1936, African American runner Jesse Owens captured four medals at the Olympic Games in Munich, much to the chagrin of Germany's dictator, Adolph Hitler.

- The dirigible airship Hindenburg caught fire and crashed in New Jersey on May 6, 1937.

♦ After four years of construction, The Golden Gate Bridge opened on May 27, 1937. The 8,980-foot-long span connects the San Francisco Bay and the Pacific Ocean.

♦ Germany ignited World War II when they invaded Poland on September 1, 1939.

Some important stuff that happened in Major League Baseball in the 1930s:

♦ In 1930, Bill Terry of the New York Giants collected 254 hits for a .401 batting average.

♦ With the Great Depression in full swing in the 1930s, attendance at Major League baseball games dropped an average of 13 percent when compared to the 1920s.

♦ Legendary manager John McGraw retired on June 1, 1932, and handed the reigns of the Giants over to first baseman Bill Terry. McGraw finished with a lifetime managerial record of 2,583 wins and 1,948 losses.

♦ After being released by the New York Yankees following the 1934 season, one-time slugging great Babe Ruth signed a contract with the Boston Braves. Out-of-shape and plagued by sore legs, Ruth fizzled in 1935 (.181 AVG, 6 HR) and retired days after playing in the first game of a Memorial Day doubleheader.

♦ In April 1934, the Phillies and the Pirates were the last clubs to play home games on Sundays.

♦ Crosley Field in Cincinnati is the scene of the first night game in major league history when the Reds hosted the Phillies on May 24, 1935.

♦ A late-season 21 game winning streak catapulted the Chicago Cubs to the 1935 NL pennant.

♦ After placing 2nd in 1935, the Yankees won another pennant in 1936. Hall-of-Famer Joe DiMaggio debuted for the Bombers with a .323 AVG, 29 HR, and 125 RBI.

♦ Left-hander Johnny Vander Meer of the Reds pitches two consecutive no-hitters in June 1938.

♦ *On May 2, 1939, Yankee first baseman Lou Gehrig pulled himself from the starting line-up after he appeared in a then-record 2,130 consecutive games. A muscular disease known as Amyotrophic Lateral Sclerosis (ALS) robbed him of the ability to hit and field well. The malady eventually claimed Gehrig's life in 1941.

◆ ◆ ◆

Hey, you Hep Cats! Check out these "I Am Not a Baseball Bozo" Award winners and "Honorable Mention" selections for the 1930s:

1930 Phil Todt *(Boston Red Sox 52-102)*. It was a satisfactory year at the plate (.269 AVG, 11 HR, 62 RBI) but another great year with the glove, finishing with a .993 fielding percentage (2nd best in AL). A low .312 OBP prevents Todt from securing another INBB, but his overall steady work warranted an Honorable Mention.

1930 Tom Oliver *(Boston Red Sox)*. As bad as they were, the Red Sox were fortunate enough to have some guys who did a pretty good job of catching the ball and not screwing up plays in the field. Otherwise, they might have lost even more games. Oliver led AL centerfielders in fielding percentage (.982) and putouts (477). No slouch with the stick, the man from Alabama nicknamed "Rebel" finished with a .293 AVG that included 34 doubles.

1930 Earl Webb *(Boston Red Sox)*. Solid stats for the 32-year-old outfielder earned him the soon-to-be coveted INBB Award. He led Boston in AVG (.323), OBP (.385), HR (16), and RBI (66). He also hit 30 doubles and six triples.

Speaking of two-baggers, Webb set the all-time record (that still stands) for doubles in a season when he ripped 67 in 1931.

1930 Milt Gates *(Boston Red Sox)*. Offensive stats began to rise in the 1920s and continued to climb in the 1930s. Some of the reasons cited for the increase are a) banning the spitball and other "doctored" pitches, b) a new game ball in use with tighter stitching (although baseball officials denied this—players were certain that the ball had been made livelier, and c) the practice of introducing "fresh" baseballs into the game regularly. Before 1920, a game ball might be utilized for the entire contest, even if it was scuffed and darkened by repeated use. Cleaner baseballs were harder for pitchers to doctor and easier for batters to see.

I mention all this to point out that the Red Sox staff ERA in 1930 of 4.68 was the *third-best in the AL*. However, the Committee isn't impressed and believes that an ERA of 4.68 is crappy and undeserving of any kudos just for being better than five other pitching staffs.

If you ask me, that Committee is a *sharp* bunch.

Beantown hurler Milt Gaston distinguished himself with 13 wins, 3.92 ERA, 1.355 WHIP, and 21 complete games. Honorable Mention.

1930 A Bunch of Guys *(Philadelphia Phillies 52-102)*. Unless you just picked this book up and started reading here randomly, you know everything you need to know about the Phillies' home park, Baker Bowl. If you're new to the discussion, go back and read the write-ups about Phillies honorees in the 1920s. That should explain everything.

With pertinent overall and road stats listed, the following guys deserved INBBs:

Chuck Klein (.386 AVG, .436 OBP, 40 HR, 170 RBI overall; .332 AVG, .391 OBP, 14 HR, 61 RBI road).

Lefty O'Doul (.383 AVG, .453 OBP, 22 HR, 97 RBI overall; .363 AVG, .427 OBP, 9 HR, 46 RBI road).

Don Hurst (.327 AVG, .401 OBP, 17 HR, 78 RBI overall; .307 AVG, .384 OBP, 8 HR, 45 RBI road).

Pinky Whitney (.342 AVG, .383 OBP, 117 RBI overall; .318 AVG, .350 OBP, 50 RBI road).

Barney Friberg (.341 AVG, .425 OBP overall; .328 AVG, .411 OBP road).

Philly's pitching staff was worthless with a combined 6.71 ERA except to offer extra batting practice to opposing teams.

1931 No 100 loss teams.

1932 Smead Jolley *(Boston Red Sox 43-111)*. Through the season-long catastrophe, Jolley remained jolly with a .309 AVG, .345 OBP, 18 HR, and 99 RBI.

Sort Of Random Trivia: Move over Rogers and Hammerstein! Did you know that the authors of the diamond classic "Take Me Out to The Ballgame" *never* attended a baseball game? Sounds a little unbelievable, but this sort of thing has happened before. For example, the composer of those classic surf songs recorded by the Beach Boys, Brian Wilson, *never* rode a surfboard, either.

1932 Dale Alexander *(Boston Red Sox)*. Alexander played part of the 1932 season with the Tigers. Between the two clubs, the first baseman captured the AL batting title with a .367 AVG and finished 3rd in OBP (.454). Alexander was playing well in 1933 when he injured a leg sliding into home plate. The Red Sox trainer used brand-new technology, a diathermy machine, to reduce the pain and swelling. The apparatus was left on too long and severely burned the player's leg, forcing an early retirement.

"They just barbecued his leg," his son Don said later.

1932 Ed Durham *(Boston Red Sox)*. On a staff that registered a collectively rancid 5.02 ERA, Durham's mark of 3.80 looks positively wonderful. His 1.391 WHIP comes across as incredible when compared to the mucho dismal club mark of 1.605. The man richly deserves the deceptively precious INBB Award bestowed upon him by the august and discerning members of the Committee.

(Isn't hyperbole wonderful? It's the stuff baseball writing dreams are made of!)

Durham was another quality player on the Red Sox roster to have his career cut short by an injury. The onset of arm miseries in 1934 limited the lefty's ability to pitch, and after several attempts at a comeback, Durham decided to retire in 1936.

1932 Ivy Andrews *(Boston Red Sox)*. INBB worthy stats for Ivy, who also pitched for the Yankees the first couple months of the season (10-7 record, 3.52 ERA, 1.359 WHIP).

Sort-of Random Trivia: Believe it or not, Andrews' nickname was "Poison." I was a little confused at first, but now I think I get it . . .

1933 Yes, Virginia, there were no 100 loss clubs.

1934 None in 1934 either, but the Reds and the White Sox tried hard, losing 99 games each.

1935 Wally Berger *(Boston Braves)*. Berger was one of baseball's elite players. He led the NL in HR (34) and RBI (130), plus his .548 slugging percentage was 4th best in the league. Berger covered a lot of ground in the outfield, leading Senior Circuit centerfielders in putouts with 411.

1935 Tommy Thompson *(Boston Braves)*. He played all three outfield positions, batted .273, and drove in 39 runs in 343 plate appearances. Honorable Mention.

1936 Lou Finney *(Philadelphia A's 53-100)*. By the mid-1930s, first basemen were supposed to be power guys who drilled lots of home runs and knocked in bushels of baserunners. Finney was an exception, his season-high in homers was ten, but he did a lot of other things well. In 1936, his fine .287 average included 26 doubles and ten triples. Finney led the AL in at-bats and only struck out 22 times, so he was getting the bat on the ball regularly. A mobile first sacker, he finished the season with the 2nd highest range factor in the league (10.46). The fella with the unusual middle name "Klopsche" also put in more-than-few innings in the outfield for Connie Mack and didn't embarrass himself.

Can you spell "INBB"?

And no fair looking it up!

1936 Pinky Higgins *(Philadelphia A's)*. Not to be confused with the "Pinky" who handled third base for the Phillies (Whitney) earlier in the decade, third-sacker Higgins wins an INBB for his work during another Titanic-like season for the A's. His .289 AVG, .366 OBP, 12 HR, and 32 doubles look mighty good on a club that finished last in the AL in several batting categories.

1936 Wally Moses *(Philadelphia A's)*. Even Moses' .345 batting average was unable to lead the White Elephants to the Promised Land of the first division.

(Sorry, I couldn't resist the allusion to the *Old Testament*.)

Moses was a solid and aggressive player who lost quite a few games during his 17-year career due to injuries from crashing into outfield walls. INBB for one of manager Mack's all-time favorite players.

1936 George Puccinelli *(Philadelphia A's)*. His major league career was a brief four years. He might have hung around longer but had trouble catching balls in the outfield.

"I would have kept him another season had it not been for his uncertainty in covering right field. He tried his hardest to make good, and I am sorry he has to go," Connie Mack said after selling Puccinelli to a minor league team.

The gentleman nicknamed "Count" could hit a little, and his line in 1936 warranted an INBB despite his fielding woes (.278 AVG, .369 OBP, 11 HR, 30 doubles, and 78 RBI).

1936 Bob Johnson *(Philadelphia A's)*. An eight-time All-Star, Johnson was the main power source in the A's line-up from 1933-1942. The righty slugger garnered the "Big Enchilada" for work during a typical season for him (.292 AVG, .389 OBP, 25 HR, 121 RBI).

1936 Chubby Dean *(Philadelphia A's)*. Alfred Lovell Dean had an interesting career. He was a backup first baseman and pinch-hitter for the A's for a couple of seasons. The man must have had a great arm because, by 1938, desperate for anything that remotely resembled major league pitching, the A's began to use him almost exclusively as a pitcher. Dean never distinguished himself as a hurler (lifetime ERA 5.08 over 686 innings), but neither did almost everyone else who pitched for the A's at the time.

A rookie and non-pitcher in 1936, the Chubster appeared in 111 games, hit .287, and fielded .989. "Pretty good," my Aunt Millie would often say. Uncle Rufus would always reply, "Pretty good ain't good at all."

I'm sticking with Aunt Millie. Dean gets an INBB.

Sorry, Uncle Rufus.

1936 Harry Kelley *(Philadelphia A's)*. Mr. McGillicuddy's staff ace snared an INBB with a 15-12 record, 3.86 ERA, 1.381 WHIP, and 20 complete games.

1936 Dolph Camilli *(Philadelphia Phillies 54-100)*. I realize that this book is designed to be heavy on the stats, but to do Baker Bowl/road performance comparisons *again* would bog things down. Suffice to say, the following honorees compiled, at the very least, decent stats on the road as well as at home. Look those numbers up if you need to, but you can trust me.

Camilli finished 2nd in the NL in home runs (28) and 5th in RBI (102). His batting average (.315) wasn't too shabby, either.

1936 Pinky Whitney *(Philadelphia Phillies)*. We need to get our Pinkys in order here. *This* Pinky is the same guy who played for the Phillies in the early part of the decade. The *other* Pinky, who played for the A's (Higgins), was traded to Detroit in the off-season. Got it?

The newly acquired Pinky (Whitney) delivered good stuff (.294 AVG, .354 OBP, 59 RBI).

1936 Chuck Klein *(Philadelphia Phillies)*. One of the greatest players to ever wear a Phillies uniform, he began the season with the Cubs and was traded back to the Phils in May. . Not the force he was earlier in his career, Klein still presented a difficult obstacle for opposing pitchers (.309 AVG, .352 OBP, 20 HR, 86 RBI). A 2nd INBB Award goes to the future Hall of Fame inductee.

1936 Johnny Moore *(Philadelphia Phillies)*. Veteran lefty swinger compensated for mediocre outfield glove work (.948) with a potent bat (.328 AVG, .365 OBP, 16 HR, 68 RBI).

1936 Lou Chiozza *(Philadelphia Phillies)*. Back in the 1960s, the Phillies had a player named Cookie Rojas, who played every position on the field and did a good job wherever he was placed. The ultimate "utility man," Rojas even pitched a few innings for manager Gene Mauch. He was no slouch at the plate, either, registering career-high batting averages of .291 and .303 during two of his seven years in Philadelphia.

Lou Chiozza was sort of an early version of Rojas; you could plug him into the infield or outfield, and he'd do an adequate job for you. Also, like Cookie, Lou was respectable with the bat. In 1936, his .297 average included 32 doubles and six triples. He also led the Phils in stolen bases with 17. The Committee decided the most "respectable" thing they could do is award Chiozza an INBB.

1936 Claude Passeau *(Philadelphia Phillies)*. In his first full season in the big leagues, Passeau established himself as one of the best hurlers in the

NL. Winner of 11 games, his 3.48 ERA was 1.16 runs per game, lower than the team's composite figure. Perhaps his most incredible stat was the mere seven home runs he surrendered over 217 innings pitched while making half of his appearances in homer-friendly Baker Bowl. INBB.

1937 Harlond Clift *(St. Louis Browns 46-108)*. It was an All-Star-type season for one of the least-remembered stars of the 1930s. While toiling in the obscurity of another Browns dumpster fire of a season, Clift slammed 29 home runs, knocked in 118, and scored 103. No need to mention his .306 batting average and .413 on-base percentage to prove the man deserved an INBB Award.

Sort of Random Trivia: Phillies great Robin Roberts once threw a perfect game of sorts. On May 13, 1954, Roberts started against the Reds and gave up a lead-off home run to Bobby Adams. The Hall-of-Fame righty then proceeded to retire the next 27 batters with no runners of any kind. The Phils won the game 8-1.

1937 Sam West *(St. Louis Browns)*. West was the starting left fielder for the AL in the 1937 All-Star Game. He could hit (.329 AVG, .390 OBP, 37 doubles) and was an excellent outfielder, finishing 2nd in the league in fielding percentage (.983) and putouts (442).

1937 Beau Bell, et al. *(St. Louis Browns)*. As is true of many bad teams, the Browns major trouble was not their offensive attack. They had guys on their roster, like outfielder Beau Bell, who could swing the bat. His impressive line looks like this: .340 AVG, .391 OBP, 14 HR, 117 RBI, 51 2B, eight 3B. Pardon the cliché, but the proverbial "icing on the (INBB) cake" was the man's stellar work with the glove. Bell led Junior Circuit right fielders in fielding percentage (.981) and ALL outfielders in assists with 22. He, too, was a member of the 1937 American League All-Star team.

Teammates Joe Vosmik (.323 AVG, .377 OBP, 93 RBI), Ethan Allen (.316 AVG, .360 OBP), and Harry Davis (.276 AVG, .374 OBP) all played well enough to join Bell in winning top honors.

The Browns' pitching staff—FORGET ABOUT IT!

1938 Hersh Martin *(Philadelphia Phillies 45-105)*. Finally, no more explanations about Baker Bowl. This was the year the Phils moved into Shibe

Park, so we no longer need to consider how the cozy confines of the Bowl often inflated the team's overall stats. The Committee is quite appreciative as it means they no longer need to put in long hours dissecting those numbers and can now spend more time with loved ones, friends, and hobbies.

This book is, if anything, is a family-friendly venture.

What about Hersh Martin? Well, he copped an INBB for a .298 AVG,347 OBP, and 36 doubles. The rest of the league was impressed, too, and selected him to the NL All-Star squad. Martin also received a bit of support for league MVP honors.

1938 Morrie Arnovich *(Philadelphia Phillies)*. Nicknamed "Snooker" because of his outstanding ability in British-style pocket billiards, Arnovich was also proficient at playing baseball. While most of his team was swirling down the sewer, the outfielder hit a nifty .275 and led the team in RBI with 72.

(I was wondering, did billiards legend Minnesota Fats play baseball? And if he did, was he any good at it?)

1939 Heinie Mueller *(Philadelphia Phillies)*. A "jack-of-all-trades" for manager Doc Protho, Mueller could be used both as an infielder or outfielder. At the plate, Mueller enjoyed the best season of his career (.279 AVG, .342 OBP, 43 RBI). He also hit nine homers to tie Joe Marty for the club lead. Not exactly great stats, but the Phillies *really* stank in 1939, finishing dead last in the league in hits, runs scored, batting average, and home runs. Compared to the major league imposters wearing Phillies uniforms that surrounded him, Mueller's numbers stood out. INBB.

1939 Syl Johnson *(Philadelphia Phillies)*. I can't blame the ballpark for Philly's terrible pitching performances (5.17 ERA, 1.569 WHIP). The grizzled 38-year-old veteran tried to show his mound mates how it's supposed to be done (3.81 ERA, 1.144 WHIP), but that was like trying to get Elvis to cut out the late-night pizza and peanut butter and banana sandwich binges.

It wasn't gonna happen.

Phillies outfielder Chuck Klein. He swung a potent bat both at Baker Bowl and on-the-road. (Courtesy Goudey Gum Company)

Lefty O'Doul got on-base at a .453 clip during the hit-happy 1930 season. (Courtesy Goudey Gum Company)

The winner of the 1932 AL batting title with a .367 AVG, Dale Alexander. (Courtesy *The Sporting News*)

Twenty-one complete games in 1930 help pitcher Milt Gaston secure an Honorable Mention. (Courtesy Library of Congress)

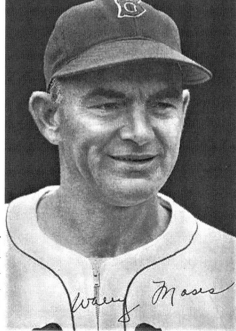

Wally Moses was an aggressive player that played hard and performed well on some of the worst teams in baseball history. (Courtesy Boston Red Sox via tradingcarddb.com)

38-year-old Syl Johnson posted a sparkling 1.144
WHIP in 1939. (Courtesy Library of Congress)

The prohibition against the manufacture, sale, and consumption of alcohol in
the United States ended on December 5, 1933. (Courtesy Library of Congress)

Browns' slugging third baseman Harlond Clift.
(Courtesy Bowman Gum)

One of history's greatest aviation disasters took place in May 1937 when the dirigible
Hindenburg exploded.

The 1940s

We'll Meet Again

Some important stuff that happened in the 1940s:

- April-May 1940. World War II intensified when German armies invaded Norway, Denmark, Holland, Belgium, France, and Luxembourg.

- On December 7, 1941, Japan launched a sneak attack on the U.S. Naval base at Pearl Harbor, Hawaii. As a result, the U.S. declared war on Japan and Germany, and Germany declared war on the United States.

- The classic film *Casablanca* premiered in November 1942. Starring Humphrey Bogart and Ingrid Bergman, it is considered by some the greatest movie of all-time.

- The first musical written by Rodgers and Hammerstein, *Oklahoma!*, opened on Broadway. The date was March 31, 1943.

- The largest seaborne invasion in history began on June 6, 1944, as hundreds of thousands of U.S. and allied soldiers assaulted German forces embedded at and near the beaches of Normandy, France.

- Franklin Roosevelt, the only person to be elected President of the United States more than two times, overwhelmingly won a 4th term in office on November 7, 1941. He would die 88 days later and be succeeded by his Vice-President, Harry S. Truman.

- The European theater of World War II ended in May 1945 when Germany surrendered to Allied forces.

- After U.S. atomic bombs destroyed the cities of Hiroshima and Nagasaki, Japan surrendered on August 15, 1945, bringing an end to World War II.

- In August 1949, Russia successfully tested their first atomic bomb at a test site in Kazakhstan.

- Mao Zedong, after he led Chinese Communist forces to victory over the armies of the Nationalist regime, declared the founding of The People's Republic of China on October 1, 1949.

Some important stuff that happened in Major League Baseball in the 1940s:

- From May 15 to July 16, 1941, Yankee outfielder Joe DiMaggio hit in a record 56 straight games, a mark that eclipsed the previous streak of 44 games set by Wee Willie Keeler in 1897.

- On the last day of the 1941 season, Ted Williams of the Red Sox went six for eight in a doubleheader against the A's and finished with a .406 batting average. As of 2021, there has not been a major league player to hit .400 or higher since.

- Early in 1942, U.S. President Roosevelt gave the "green light" for baseball to continue to play even though the country is embroiled in World War II.

- On May 22, 1942, Ted Williams joined hundreds of major league baseball players who served in the U.S. military during the Second World War. The steady exodus of major leaguers severely reduced the quality of play through1945 and into the first few weeks of the 1946 campaign.

- Founded by chewing gum magnate Philip K. Wrigley, the All-American Girls Professional Baseball League (AAGPBL) began operation in 1943. Remember, there is no crying in baseball!

- For years, an American League doormat, The St. Louis Browns, captured the 1944 pennant in a close race with the Detroit Tigers. The crosstown rival Cardinals defeated the "Brownies" four games to two in the World Series.

- Major League baseball's "color line" ended when African American Jackie Robinson took the field for the first time as a Brooklyn Dodger in April 1947.

- The Cleveland Indians became the 2nd major league club to integrate in 1947 when they added hard-hitting outfielder Larry Doby to their roster.

- On August 16, 1948, Hall of Famer Babe Ruth died at 53 at Memorial Sloan Kettering Cancer Center in New York.

- Phillies veteran Eddie Waitkus was shot and nearly killed by a deranged female fan on June 14, 1949. Almost miraculously, Waitkus recovered and was Philly's starting first baseman during the 1950 campaign.

◆ ◆ ◆

These fellas "cooked with gas" playing for tail-ender dog teams in the 1940s and qualified for INBBs and Honorable Mentions.

1940 Frankie Hayes *(Philadelphia A's 54-100)*. Back in those days, it must have been tough to be a Philadelphia baseball fan. Both the Phillies and Connie Mack's bunch were dreadfully bad. Both clubs would become competitive in the later years of the decade, but there wasn't much to cheer about during those early seasons.

Frankie Hayes gave the hardy few who ventured to Shibe Park something to smile about. He hit .308. compiled a .389 OBP, launched 16 HR, and drove in 70. He even led the team in steals with nine.

1940 Wally Moses *(Philadelphia A's)*. INBB number two for Moses. A real ball hawk, he led all AL right fielders in putouts seven times (1937, 1938, 1940, 1941, 1943, 1944, 1945). *The Sporting News* said, "If a spectacular dive over the turf is necessary to snare a fly ball seemingly out of his reach, Wally dives."

The man from Uvalda, Georgia, impressed with the bat, too, rocking 1940 with a .309 BA, .396 OBP, 41 doubles, and nine triples.

1940 Bob Johnson *(Philadelphia A's)*. It was Johnson's second INBB, as well. His batting average was an OK .268 but his OBP an excellent .374. Add thirty-one dingers and 103 ribbies, and you got the recipe for an IBB Award. Two thumbs-up and a hearty pat-on-the-back!

1940 Dick Seibert *(Philadelphia A's)*. His OBP (.325) could be slightly higher, but on a team that collectively batted .262, the Committee likes the .286 AVG, 31 doubles, and 77 RBI. Did someone say "INBB"?

1940 Sam Chapman *(Philadelphia A's)*. Trouble getting on base wasn't what haunted the 100-loss A's the most in 1940. Making the plays they needed to make in the field was a weak spot. They made the most errors (238) in the league to finish dead-last finish in fielding percentage (.960). It's true, Wally Moses was a good fielder, but he was one of a few exceptions.

What does this have to do with Sam Chapman? After thoughtful discussion, the Commission feels that Chapman's season typifies part-of-the-reason why the A's struggled. He posted decent numbers at the plate (.276 BA, 23 HR, and 75 RBI), but his fielding left a lot to be desired. His 14 miscues led all Junior Circuit centerfielders. Joining him in the inept glove work department were A's leftfielder Bob Johnson who managed a mediocre fielding percentage (.959), and Dick Siebert, who led AL first sackers in errors with 22.

Despite Chapman's fielding challenges, he gets an INBB for a significant contribution to the offense with 23 HR and 75 RBI.

1940 Johnny Babich *(Philadelphia A's)*. As bad as Philadelphia's fielding was, their pitching was worse. The team ERA was an astronomical (5.22) and WHIP an excessive (1.544). Only two gents distinguished themselves, Babich and Bill Beckman.

Here's Babich's INBB Award-winning line: (14-13, 3.73 ERA, 1.317 WHIP, 16 complete games).

Beckman was mainly a relief pitcher. Although his ERA wasn't good (4.17), he did post an 8-4 record and 1.312 WHIP. Honorable Mention.

1940 Pinky May *(Philadelphia Phillies 50-103)*. The father of future major league catcher Milt May was solid again with the bat (.293 BA, .371 OBP) but was shaky as a third baseman (.954 fielding percentage). As you probably realize already, a high OBP covers a multitude of sins with the Committee. The "other" Pinky (not Higgins) gets another one of those wonderful INBBs.

1940 Johnny Rizzo *(Philadelphia Phillies)*. He started the season with the Pirates, was dealt to the Reds, and then shipped to the Phillies in June. Ending up on a perpetual tailender could have been enough to depress anyone totally, but Rizzo was made of sterner stuff. He hit 24 home runs for the entire season, 20 of which were propelled while in a Phillies uniform. Following the trade, his batting average was .292 and OBP .358. Who could possibly argue with an INBB for John Costa Rizzo?

1940 Kirby Higbe *(Philadelphia Phillies)*. Good pitcher with the misfortune of pitching for one of the worst teams in baseball history for a couple of seasons. Dodger General Manager Larry McPhail thought the man had the best curve ball in baseball. Higbe managed to win 14 games and put up a 3.72 ERA and 1.283 WHIP, and earned an All-Star berth in 1940.

1940 Hugh Mulcahy *(Philadelphia Phillies)*. The now-famous nickname of "Losing Pitcher Mulcahy" can almost entirely be attributed to the misfortune of playing for some very pathetic teams. Mulcahy wasn't a great pitcher or even a good one, but he usually did a satisfactory job and gave the manager lots of innings. 1940 was one of his best seasons (13 wins, 3.60 ERA, 1.336 WHIP, 21 complete games). Mulcahy had the distinction of being the first major leaguer to be drafted by Uncle Sam into military service in World War II.

1941 Nick Etten *(Philadelphia Phillies 43-111)*. The Phillies again, huh? Yep, they wuz *terrible*. Fortunately for Shibe Park diehards, there were occasional glimpses of major league quality baseball. For example, first baseman Nick Etten had a season that would make any mother proud (even Frank Zappa)! Through the carnage, he hit .311, clouted 14 home runs, and plated 79 of his teammates.

1941 Danny Litwhiler *(Philadelphia Phillies)*. A steady performer who deserved better, Litwhiler clubbed 18 home runs, knocked in 66, and batted .305. One of the best left fielders in baseball, he led the NL in putouts (327) and assists (13). The Cardinals thought he was a darn good player and would acquire Litwhiler in 1943 to help their push to an eventual pennant and World Series.

1941 Pinky May *(Philadelphia Phillies)*. Honorable Mention. May got off to a slow start, batting way below .200 in his first 100 at-bats but caught fire and finished with a .267 average. He didn't have a lot of extra-base hits, but at least he was getting on base at a decent clip (.344) and his fielding percentage improved to .972.

1941 Joe Marty *(Philadelphia Phillies)*. Marty posted Honorable Mention-worthy numbers (.264 AVG, .344 OBP, eight HR). As a member of the

Cubs in 1938, Marty went to the plate 12 times during the World Series, smacked a homer, drove in five runs, and batted .500.

It took a lot of doin' to lose 111 games and the Phillies' pitching staff done did their bit to hasten the plunge to those depths. Do I need to cite the numbers? Suffice to say, the team finished with the worst ERA in the league, allowed the most hits, earned runs, and walks. Sadly, there's even more abysmal stuff, but I'd rather not turn this section into the literary equivalent of rubber necking at the scene of a bad accident. Let us turn our heads away and keep moving forward.

1942 Nick Etten (*Philadelphia Phillies 42-109*). When talking about himself to other players, the 6'2", 200-pound Etten liked to refer to himself as "Big Nick." Well, the large man's line wasn't quite worthy of an INBB (we have *very* high standards), but his .264 AVG, .357 OBP, eight HR, and 21 doubles are more than enough to pick up an Honorable Mention.

1942 Danny Litwhiler *Philadelphia Phillies*). A year away from his liberation to the Cardinals, Danny batted .271, hit nine HR, 25 doubles, and nine triples. His OBP was mediocre (.310), but he was flawless with the glove, handling 317 chances with no errors for a fielding percentage of 1.000. With the positives outweighing the one negative, Litwhiler captured another INBB.

1942 Tommy Hughes *(Philadelphia Phillies)*. Although the Phils' staff finished last in the league in ERA with a 4.12 figure, 4.12 isn't *super* bad. Several hurlers counter-balanced the yuckiness of teammates that posted earned-run averages like 4.94, 5.20, 5.69, and 6.12. The following Phillies pitchers weren't "Phutile" and merited INBBs:

1. Tommy Hughes (12 wins, 3.06 ERA, 1.277 WHIP, 19 complete games).
2. Syl Johnson (8 wins, 3.69 ERA, 1.382 WHIP, 10 complete games). THAT'S A THIRD INBB FOR SYLVESTER! YOWZZZAR!
3. Johnny Podgajny (6 wins, 3.61 ERA, 1.361 WHIP).

And because his WHIP was a rather high 1.404, Rube Melton cops just an Honorable Mention (instead of an INBB) for winning nine games and recording a 3.70 ERA.

1943 Jo Jo White *(Philadelphia A's 49-105)*. Born Joyner Clifford White in the tiny town of Red Oak, Georgia, he spoke with the sort of southern drawl you'd expect.

"He was called Jo-Jo because of the way he pronounced his native state," one-time Tiger teammate Hank Greenberg explained.

Sir Paul McCartney once said, "Jo Jo was a man who thought he was a loner," but I seriously doubt that the former Beatle ever saw the man play baseball.

A serviceable, non-spectacular player, Jo-Jo secured an Honorable Mention for playing relatively well in 1943. A .248 average and .335 OBP included seven triples, and his 12 stolen bases tied for the club lead.

Get back, Jo Jo!

1943 Bobby Estalella *(Philadelphia A's)*. The team collectively hit .232, so Estalella's .259 BA looks good. He cracked 11 home runs and drove in 63 to lead the A's in both categories. Competent with the glove, he committed only 6 errors over 854 innings played.

I bet you agree with the Committee that Estella deserves an INBB Award.

You do, don't you?

1943 Jesse Flores *(Philadelphia A's)*. The first big league pitcher to be born in Mexico, Flores grabbed the top honor with a line that included 12 wins, 3.11 ERA, and 1.202 WHIP. The 175- pound right-hander later gained distinction as one of the finest scouts in the majors.

1943 Roger Wolff *(Philadelphia A's)*. As a member of the Pirates, Mr. Wolff wrapped up his seven-year career with two scoreless innings of relief against the Dodgers on August 25, 1947. The significance of that date is that I was born exactly ten years later.

Interesting, huh?

In 1943, Roger toiled for Connie Mack's pitiful A's. A real gamer, he battled any discouragement he might have felt pitching for a flock of turkeys to win 10 games, register a 3.54 ERA and 1.376 WHIP. Two thumbs-up and a virtual pat-on-the-back for Roger!

1943 Russ Christopher *(Philadelphia A's)*. Let's keep it simple for this one; Christopher wins an INBB (In 133 innings pitched a 3.45 ERA and 1.338 WHIP).

1944 Nobody lost 100 or more ball games. The Senators dropped 90, the Dodgers 91, and the Phillies gave up the ghost "only" 92 times.

1945 Vince DiMaggio *(Philadelphia Phillies 46-108)*. He was no Joe DiMaggio (or even a Dom), but the "forgotten" DiMaggio put up some good stats during his time as a big leaguer. In 1945, he slammed 19 home runs, knocked in 84, and led the Phils in steals with 12. An excellent glove man, DiMaggio finished with the 2nd best fielding percentage in the NL (.994) and 4th in outfield assists (16).

1945 Vance Dinges *(Philadelphia Phillies)*. After toiling for seven years in the minors, the 30-year-old Dinges finally got a chance in the Big Show with the Phillies. The outfielder-first baseman made the most of the opportunity by batting .287 and slugging 17 home runs in only 440 plate appearances. He'd be back in the minors a couple of years later when the guys who went to war started coming back in full force, but for a while, Dinges was one of the best players on the Phillies.

1945 Andy Karl *(Philadelphia Phillies)*. Once again, Philly's pitching staff was a catastrophe, finishing last in ERA (4.64), hits allowed (1546), runs allowed (864), and walks issued (608). Closer Andy Karl was one of only two hurlers to thrive among the ruins (2.99 ERA, 1.245 WHIP, a league-leading15 saves over 67 appearances).

Number four man in the starting rotation, Dick Mauney made the folks in his hometown of Concord, North Carolina, proud with a 3.08 ERA and 1.255 WHIP over 123 innings pitched. The INBB Award Committee isn't proud, as none of the members hail from Georgia, but they think stats like that are, well, really *swell*.

1946 Elmer Valo *(Philadelphia A's 49-105)*. Old-time comedian W.C. Fields liked to poke fun at Philadelphia. The virtually hopeless Phillies and A's baseball squads during the era might have partially inspired Fields' jocular lampooning of the City of Brotherly Love. (Keep in mind that part of my responsibility as an author is to write things that make you think, even if those things seem stupid or irrelevant.)

After serving in the military for two-and-a-half years, Elmer Valo returned to the A's in high style, batting a sizzling .354 with a lofty .433 OBP. He avoided crashing into any outfield walls during the season to handle 194 chances with only five errors committed. Elmer was also the top base stealer on the team with nine pilfers.

1946 Sam Chapman *(Philadelphia A's)*. After three years in the U.S. Navy, Chapman proved he still had his baseball mojo going with 20 HR and 67 RBI. Too bad most of the rest of the A's played like they were hexed by a malevolent entity . . .

1946 Buddy Rosar *(Philadelphia A's)*. Even though Rosar was named to the All-Star team and received a few votes for league MVP, the Committee isn't overly enthralled with his .283 BA and .339 OBP. . Over 446 plate appearances, the catcher only swatted two home runs and knocked in 47, not exactly stellar statistics. The numbers are good enough, however, for an Honorable Mention.

1946 Phil Marchildon *(Philadelphia A's)*. As a member of the Royal Canadian Air Force, the bomber Marchildon was flying in was shot down in 1944. He survived the crash and was captured by the Germans, who sent him to a concentration camp where he spent nine terrible months. Before the war, Marchildon had been friendly and gregarious, but things changed.

"Phil really changed after his war experiences," a teammate said, "he was very serious and rarely spoke about what he had gone through.

According to available information, the right-handed pitcher never recovered emotionally and mentally from his war-time ordeal.

Physically, he was able to pitch effectively again. Marchildon's INBB Award-winning line for 1946: 13-16, 3.49 ERA, 1.372 WHIP, 16 complete games.

1946 Dick Fowler *(Philadelphia A's)*. The lanky Canadian (6'4") finished with a 9-16 record, but with a better team, those numbers probably would have been reversed. His ERA was good (3.28), and he completed 14 games. Fowler would win 42 more over the next three seasons and was a key player in the A's return to respectability in the last years of the decade.

(I resisted the temptation to make a quip or pun about Fowler's last name. I figured I'd be better off winging it and flying into the next award winner without delay).

1946 Jesse Flores *(Philadelphia A's)*. Connie Mack's Mexican mound mae-stro did it again with an INBB-worthy 9-7 record, 2.32 ERA, and 1.194 WHIP. Ole'!

1947 No humiliating 100 or more loss campaigns.

1948 Luke Appling *(Chicago White Sox 51-101)*. I find it refreshing to write about players on a team besides the A's and Phillies. The 41-year-old Appling split time between third base and shortstop. Defensively, he was a negative, leading all AL infielders in errors with 35. However, his bat work was a different story (.314 BA, .423 OBP). Those old legs managed to steal ten bases, the second-highest total on the club.

1948 Dave Philley *(Chicago White Sox)*. Tough-as-nails player who never walked away from a fight. "I play so hard to win that if a man gets in my way, I go into him, knock him down," he once told an interviewer.

There were two tiers to his career, one as a productive everyday player (1946–1956) and the other as one-of-the best pinch hitters in baseball history (1957–1962). Philley focused during Chicago's blow-out 101 loss season, turning in a .287 BA and .353 OBP. More than adequate with the glove, his overall fielding percentage was 3rd best in the league (.979), and he led all AL centerfielders in assists with 21.

1948 Taffy Wright *(Chicago White Sox)*. The top fielding right fielder in the league in 1948 with a .986 percentage, Taft Sheldon Wright added a .279 BA, .341 OBP, and 61 RBI to clinch one of those wonderfully celebrated INBB Awards. And let's not forget a couple of thumbs up and a robust pat on the back!

Tax-free, of course.

1948 Randy Gumpert *(Chicago White Sox)*. When a pitching staff posts a composite 4.89 ERA, as the Pale Hose did, it's often tough to find anyone who deserves commendation. But after lots of hard digging, the Committee discovered Mr. Gumpert. Purchased from the Yankees in late July, the right-handed hurler made 11 starts and five relief appearances over the balance of the season. A 3.79 ERA, 1.192 WHIP, and six complete games justified the White Sox decision to acquire him and our decision to bestow an INBB for stellar services rendered to one sad ball club.

Sort of Random Trivia: The oldest rookie in major league baseball history was Satchel Paige. Let's have some fun—how old was the well-traveled pitcher when he broke in with the Cleveland Indians in 1948? Your choices are:

A) 86   B) 93   C) 42   D) 50

The answer can be found after the next player evaluation. Try to guess without looking it up in a book or online!

1949 Al Evans *(Washington Senators 50-104)*. When Evans began his major league career in the early 1940s, he wasn't much of a defensive catcher. His bat pretty much kept him around, but the native North Carolinian wasn't satisfied being a one-dimensional player. He worked hard to improve behind the plate and the extra effort paid off. By the end of the decade, he was one of the best defensive catchers in the league. As a matter of fact, in 1949, he led all AL receivers with a .992 fielding percentage. Evans also hit .271 with a .369 OBP.

Sort of Random Trivia ANSWER: Paige was 48. Kudos to you that guessed it correctly without consulting an outside source!

1949 Eddie Robinson *(Washington Senators)*. A fearless hitter who refused to surrender the inside of the plate, Robinson led the league in HBP and was in the top ten in that category three other times. The main power guy in the Senator's line-up, Robinson, topped the club with 18 HR and 78 RBI and made the All-Star team. No brainer INBB.

1949 Eddie Yost *(Washington Senators)*. The Awards Committee love that .383 OBP that included 91 walks. Nicknamed "The Walking Man," Yost averaged 124 walks per 162 games played over his 18-year career. His .253 BA was nothing special, but he was getting on base regularly, unlike many of his teammates. It wasn't an "empty" .253 either; of the 110 hits he recorded, 35 were for extra bases.

1949 Bud Stewart *(Washington Senators)*. Members of the Committee have successfully resisted the temptation to ask themselves, "Who the heck was Bud Stewart, and why should anyone care about what the outfielder accomplished in 1949?" Not exactly a household name, Stewart was a pretty fair ball player over a nine-year major league career, could hit a little, and didn't kill you with the glove. He enjoyed his best season in 1949, batting .284 with a .368 OBP. Not a power hitter, he did manage to hit eight home runs while playing half his games in cavernous Griffith Stadium. He handled 851 chances in the outfield and only committed four errors solidifying the case to award this virtually unknown player an INBB.

1949 Clyde Volmer *(Washington Senators)*. Members of the Committee have successfully resisted the temptation also to ask themselves, "Who the heck was Clyde Volmer, and why should anyone care about what the outfielder accomplished in 1949?" Not exactly a household name, Volmer was a pretty fair ball player over a ten-year major league career, could hit a little, and didn't kill you with the glove (Isn't "cut" and "paste" wonderful?). His .253 AVG was nothing to write home about (don't you just love clichés?), but he finished second on the Senators in HR (14) and RBI (59) behind slugger Eddie Robinson. While patrolling the outfield, he recorded a .982 fielding percentage, and that factoid solidifies the case to award this virtually unknown player an INBB.

1949 Sherry Robertson *(Washington Senators)*. Members of the Committee have successfully resisted the temptation to, yet once again, ask themselves, "Who the heck was Sherry Robertson, and why should anyone care about what the outfielder accomplished in 1949?" Not exactly a household name, Robertson was a pretty fair ball player over a ten-year major league career, could hit a little, but occasionally *killed* you with the glove. As a second baseman in 1949, he booted 20 balls and added five more miscues at third and the outfield. Robertson's bat saved him from humiliation, delivering 11 HR to go along with an almost good .329 OBP. Honorable Mention.

1949 Ray Scarborough *(Washington Senators)*. Members of the Committee have successfully resisted the temptation to ask themselves, "Who the heck was Ray Scarborough and why should anyone care about what . . ."— Awwww, gee whiz, I think I better stop it. It might have worked once or twice as a comic device, but now it's getting lame.

Scarborough was a passable hurler, lost a couple of years of his career due to military service in WW II. Sort of an early version of Murry Dickson pitched a lot of innings, generally kept his clubs in the ball game, won almost as many games as he would lose. He got an Honorable Mention for winning 13 games. A high 4.60 ERA and an elevated WHIP of 1.462 prevented Mr. Ray from winning an INBB.

1949 Roy Sievers *(St. Louis Browns)*. The 1949 American League Rookie of the Year. It was an outstanding debut season for the man nicknamed "The Squirrel." I guess there are worse nicknames, but that one isn't very flattering. Anyhow, the outfielder batted .306, got on base at a .398 clip, powered 16 home runs, and drove in 91. There's no denying that the man deserved the top acorn, er, I mean award. The Committee was just *nuts* about him and do not feel that they went out on a limb to give him the award.

1949 Sherm Lollar and associates *(St. Louis Browns)*. In studying the Browns' stats for the campaign in question, it became obvious that the team had a few players on the roster that had good seasons in 1949. This was perplexing as the Browns managed to lose 101 games. What happened? Did they have a monumental streak of bad luck? As Yul Brenner once sang in *The King and I*, "It is a puzzlement."

Seven other Brownies (besides Sievers) played well enough to earn INBB Awards for 1949. They are:

> Sherm Lollar (catcher).261 AVG, .340 OBP, 8 HR, 49 RBI in 321
> plate appearances
> Jerry Priddy (second base) .290 AVG, .382 OBP, 11 HR, 63 RBI,
> 83 runs
> Bob Dillinger (third base).324 AVG, .385 OBP, 13 HR, 20 steals
> that led the team
> Stan Spence (outfield).245 AVG, .356 OBP, 13 HR in 104 games
> Dick Kokes (outfield) .261 AVG, .351 OBP, 23 HR, 77 RBI

Jack Graham (first base) .238 AVG,,.326 OBP, 24 HR, 79 RBI

Tom Ferrick (pitcher)6-4 record, 3.88 ERA

There was also an Honorable Mention . . .

Ned Garver (pitcher)12-17, 3.98, 1.551 WHIP (thanks to 102 walks over 224 innings).

Garver won 12 games, but he was too wild to secure an outright INBB. Teammate Jack Graham's .238 batting average was poor, and OBP was a so-so .326, but his HR and RBI totals lift him into the Winner's Circle. It would be fair to question Stan Spence's award since his average wasn't too hot (.245). It was a good OBP (.356) and home run output (13) in only 104 games that sealed the deal for the lefty-swinging centerfielder.

So, how did the Browns manage to lose 101 games? As is often the case with clubs that stink, the team was done in by poor defense and pitching. St. Louis had the worst fielding percentage in the league (.972) and compiled the highest staff ERA (5.21). The pitching staff also allowed the most hits, earned runs, and home runs. Yes, the team was hitting the ball and scoring a few runs (667), but their fielding and pitching allowed a lot more (913).

In fairness, the Browns had to contend with some formidable teams that year. The Yankees had begun another dynasty and won 97 games, the Red Sox almost won the pennant with 96 victories, and the Indians (89 wins) and Tigers (87 wins) fielded strong clubs. Even the usually terrible A's finished with a good 81–73 record.

It was tough, and the Committee sympathizes.

But not too much.

Unlike many of his A's mound mates, Canadian Dick Fowler knew how to pitch and earned an INBB for the 1946 campaign. (Courtesy Bowman Gum)

41-year-old Luke Appling's compensated for an age-related decline with the glove by hitting .314. (Creative Commons)

The 1942 Phillies were so bad that even decent pitchers like Johnny Podgajny couldn't help. (Courtesy *The Sporting News*)

The 1949 AL Rookie-of-the-Year, Roy Sievers. (Courtesy Jay Publishing)

Pitchers had to throw strikes to Eddie Yost. Over his long career, he averaged 124 walks per season. (Courtesy Jay Publishing)

Frankie Hayes gave Shibe Park fans something to cheer about in 1940 with a .308 AVG and 16 HR. (Courtesy Bowman Gum)

Co-star Humphrey Bogart was a major baseball fan.

June 6, 1944: the beginning of the end for Nazi Germany. (Courtesy U.S. National Archives and Records Administration)

The 1950s

Not Everybody Can Be A Mickey Mantle

Some important stuff that happened in the 1950s:

- North Korea invaded South Korea in June. Led by the United States, the U.N. said, "You can't do that!" and intervened militarily. China eventually joined the fray on the side of North Korea, and by the time the conflict ended in 1953, approximately three million people (including citizens and military personnel) had lost their lives or were wounded.

- In June 1951, the first color TV program was broadcast on CBS. The variety show, featuring Ed Sullivan and Arthur Godfrey, was watched by practically no one as almost everyone owned black-and-white sets at the time.

- After several years of testing, a vaccine for the crippling plague of Polio developed by the labs of Dr. Jonas Salk was deemed safe for widespread use.

- The "Brown vs. The Board of Education" Decision. The U.S. Supreme Court ruled in 1954 that it was unconstitutional for states to mandate via law the racial segregation of schools.

- Elvis Presley went into the studio for the first time to record music in the summer of 1953. By 1956, he was a superstar, those swivel hips and all.

- The Space Age officially began in October 1957 when the Russians launched the world's first satellite, Sputnik.

- Legos hit the market in 1958 to the delight of children in the U.S. and the eventual chagrin of the multitudes of adults who stepped on a stray piece in their bare or stocking feet in the coming decades.

- In 1959, Fidel Castro seized power in Cuba, setting up a Communist dictatorship on that island nation. Tensions with the U.S. rose significantly; a mutual hostility almost led to a worldwide nuclear war in 1962.

Some important stuff that happened in Major League Baseball in the 1950s:

• Led by three-time MVP and future Hall-of-Famer Mickey Mantle, The New York Yankees dominated the decade, winning the World Series each year from 1949-53, and again in 1956 and 1958. Besides that, they were in the Fall Classic in 1955 and 1957.

• The Dodgers, Braves, Indians, and Giants fielded several good clubs, too. The Indians won 111 games in 1954 but were upset in the World Series by the Giants. The Dodgers were a National League powerhouse and captured pennants in 1952, 1953, 1955, 1956, and 1959. They won the World Series in 1955 and 1959. The Braves boasted a powerful lineup and stellar pitching beginning in mid-decade and earned the NL pennant and World Championship crown in 1957 and another Senior Circuit flag in 1958.

• Just four years after teammate Jackie Robinson broke baseball's color-line, Brooklyn catcher Roy Campanella became the first African American to win the MVP award (1951).

• In 1952, Phillies ace Robin Roberts won 28 games, the most victories in a season recorded by any hurler during the decade.

• After decades of playing baseball in the same cities, a series of franchise shifts disrupted the status quo. The Boston Braves moved to Milwaukee in 1953, the Browns vacated St. Louis to morph into the Baltimore Orioles in 1954, and the A's packed up and headed for Kansas City for the 1955 campaign.

• In 1958, both the Giants and Dodgers moved their operations to the West Coast. Fans of the "Jints" and the "Bums" were heartbroken.

• Legendary manager and owner of the Philadelphia As, Connie Mack, passed away at 93 in February 1956.

• The Boston Red Sox became the last Major League team to integrate when infielder Elijah Jerry "Pumpsie" Green pinch runs during a July 1959 game.

◆ ◆ ◆

Whoa, Daddy-O! Here are the winners of the "I Am Not a Baseball Bozo" Award (INBB) along with "Honorable Mention" selections for the 1950s:

1950 Ferris Fain *(Philadelphia A's 52-102)*. Not only the A's best player at the time, Fain was one of the league's elite, making the All-Star team five times and winning two batting titles. His .282 average was good, but that .430 OBP is excellent. He also drove in 83 runs for a team that finished next to last in runs scored.

1950 Elmer Valo *(Philadelphia A's)*. The man from Central Europe (Slovakia)was a reliable performer during a 20-year career. In 1950, he batted .280 (his career average was .282), got on base at a .400 clip, and led the team in stolen bases (12).

1950 Sam Chapman *(Philadelphia A's)*. Twenty-three home runs and 95 RBI earned Mack's centerfielder another INBB.

1950 Paul Lehner *(Philadelphia A's)*. Mr. Lehner posted an outstanding .309 AVG and racked up 10 assists while putting in time at all three out-field positions.

(Are you starting to wonder how a team that lost 102 games had so many players on their roster that deserve one of those magically transcendent INBB awards? If this seeming anomaly concerns you-just tell yourself that this is just a book, and everything will be alright in the end. Deep breathing exercises might help, too . . .)

1950 Lou Brissie (*Philadelphia A's* again.) Manager Mack's "ace" posted a 7-19 record, which is bad, but a 4.02 ERA isn't so terrible, and a WHIP of 1.439 was marginally OK. The war hero earns an Honorable Mention by a slim margin. This decision is based on the fact that the A's finished near the bottom of the league in errors committed and fielding percentage. Sloppy play behind Brissie may have adversely affected that won-lost record, don't you think? The Committee suspects it did and is giving the man the benefit of the doubt.

1951 Ned Garver *(St. Louis Browns 52-102)*. This was an epically *bad* team. Not only did they fail to generate a decent offense (last in the AL for runs scored, hits, batting average, on-base-percentage, and slugging), the

Browns had trouble catching the ball and making plays and finished tied with the Cubs for the worst fielding percentage (.971) in the majors.

The pitching staff was equally inept (5.18 ERA); one notable exception was right-hander Ned Garver. Somehow, Garver managed to post a 20-12 record with a 3.73 ERA and 24 complete games. This incredible performance lands the pride and joy of Ney High School in Ney, Ohio, an INBB Award. Let's hear it for Ned and good old Ney High! Rah, rah, RAH!

Sort of Random-Trivia: Tigers Pitcher Virgil Trucks struggled in 1952, losing 19 and only winning five. But twice that season, he was as "good as gold," twirling no-hitters against the Senators and Yankees.

1952 Walt Dropo *(Detroit Tigers 50-104)*. The big first baseman won an INBB with a .279 AVG, 23 HR, and 70 RBI in just 115 games. A very productive player for several years, Walt retired in 1961 after appearing in 14 games for the Orioles.

1952 Johnny Groth *(Detroit Tigers)*. Groth led the club in steals, hit .284, and posted respectable numbers (.348 OBP and 51 RBI). Expectations were high for Groth in 1949 when he became a starter and hit .293. He batted .306 and .299 the next two seasons, and then his offensive output began to decline with the 1952 campaign. Still, he had a good career (.279 average), and his work in '52 deserves two thumbs-up and a pat on the back!

1952 Ralph Kiner *(Pittsburgh Pirates 42-112)*. The Bucs were the National League's version of a punching bag in the early 1950s. Bright spots were few on this club, considered one of the all-time worst diamond ensembles. However, outfielder Ralph Kiner was no bozo and produced 37 HR and 87 RBI and a berth on the All-Star team.

1952 Gus Bell *(Pittsburgh Pirates)*. He might have won an INBB outright had his OBP been at least in the .340-.350 range (it was a low .306). His 16 home runs and 59 RBI netted him an Honorable Mention.

1952 Murray Dickson *(Pittsburgh Pirates)*. During an 18-year career, while pitching for five different teams, Dickson was the proverbial workhorse. He soaked up lots of innings and usually pitched well enough for his teams to win. Since the Pirates didn't win many games in 1952, Dickson was saddled with a league-leading 21 losses. However, he wins an INBB.

"With all those losses, why?" you ask.

Well, Dickson also won 14 and fashioned a satisfactory 3.57 ERA to go along with a fine 1.275 WHIP while pitching every fourth day for a horrible team that finished 8th (out of 8 teams) in almost every batting, pitching, and fielding statistical category. The man's work in 1952 was downright impressive, if you ask me.

(If you *didn't* ask me, I apologize. Sometimes, I get carried away with these things.)

1953 *(St. Louis Browns 54-100).* Despite the team's terrible record, five Browns deserve INBB awards. They are:

1. Vic Wertz. The lefty swinger (baseball type) drilled 19 home runs, plated 70 teammates while getting on base at a healthy .376 clip. What makes his numbers especially impressive is the fact that they were compiled in just 339 at-bats.

2. Dick Kryhoski. Before researching this book, I had never heard of the guy, so I decided to do a little research. Richard David Kryhoski played seven years in the majors and compiled a .265 career average. Primarily a first baseman, he had a little pop in his bat, socking 39 home runs from 1951-1953 as a platoon player. He was good with the glove, finishing 2nd in the AL in fielding percentage in 1951. Kryhoski hit a career-high 16 HR to go along with a .278 average and a .497 slugging percentage in 1953.

3. Dick Kokos. Another fella I never heard of. I think I'll do a little research on him, too . . .

   A native of Chicago, Illinois, Kokos wore a major league uniform from 1948-1950 and then again from 1953-1954. A lifetime .263 hitter, he could take a pitcher deep; he hit 23 home runs in 1949 and 18 in 1950. For some reason, no major or minor league stats are available for him for 1951 and 1952. I'm thinking Kokos may have been drafted and served a couple of years in the military (the Korean War broke out in 1950).

   When Kokos returned to the "Big Show" in 1953, the outfielder only hit .241 BUT had an OBP of .361 and drilled 13 home runs over 357 plate appearances. A borderline INBB winner, for sure, but that OBP cinches it. The man *was* getting on base regularly.

4. Harry Breechen. The left-handed hurler was a grizzled veteran in 1953, 38-years-old and having put in the previous 11 seasons with the cross-town Cardinals. This would be his last campaign; he retired after posting a poor 5-13 record. However, as is so often the case, the man nicknamed "The Cat" was victimized by a poor supporting cast. His ERA was quite good at 3.07, and the WHIP was a decent 1.304. The man pitched well enough to win a few more games, but the Browns were horrible, and he didn't.

5. Satchel Paige. At the age of 46, Satch posted numbers a younger man could live with (3.53 ERA, 1.304 WHIP, and 11 saves to lead the team).

1954 Cal Abrams *(Baltimore Orioles 54-100)*. It would take the Orioles a few years to develop into the powerhouse they would become in the 1960s. In the beginning, they had a few players who helped keep the fans interested and buying tickets. One of those guys was outfielder Cal Abrams. Traded from the Pirates to the Orioles in May of 1954, over 115 games he registered a .293 batting average and .400 on-base-percentage.

1954 Clint Courtney *(Baltimore Orioles)*. His .270 BA looks good on a club that collectively hit .251. As a catcher, he had a rifle arm and led the AL three years in throwing out base runners, including 37 kills in 1954.

1954 Bob Turley *(Baltimore Orioles)*. Manager Jimmy Dykes' problem that year was not his pitching staff. Turley was the ace, winning 14 games and whiffing 185 batters over 247 innings pitched. His ERA was a good 3.46. He and fellow starting pitchers Joe Coleman (13 wins, 3.50 ERA) and Duane Pillette (10 wins, 3.12 ERA) collect ever prestigious INBBs for their work.

1954 Jim Finigan *(Philadelphia A's 51-103)*. Former A's star Eddie Joost one season as a manager was a baseball nightmare. The team had managed to finish next-to-last the previous year, and there was some hope that the White Elephants might move up a couple of notches. Instead, the A's plummeted to the basement. Not everyone on the roster performed at a zombified level. Rookie third baseman Jim Finigan persevered to hit .302, which included 25 doubles and seven triples. His fielding stats weren't so great, but we won't hold that against him.

1954 Arnie Portocarreo *(Philadelphia A's).* A rookie, too, and although he lost 18 games, his line was INBB worthy (248 IP, 132 K, 16 complete games, 1.399 WHIP).

1954 Frank Thomas *(Pittsburgh Pirates 53-101).* The man nicknamed "The Big Donkey" hit 23 home runs and knocked in 94.

Thomas had a productive 16-year major league career; he powered 286 home runs and was named to three All-Star teams. He is most remembered for being involved in a famous pre-game fight with Dick Allen in 1965. Both were members of the Phillies at the time; Thomas and Allen were ribbing each other before a night game when Thomas allegedly said something that Allen thought was a racist remark. The talented rookie took exception, and a fight ensued, during which time the big first baseman struck Allen with a bat. Phillies infielder Ruben Amaro was hit with a stray punch as several teammates worked to separate the two men. The struggle was witnessed by the press and arriving fans at Connie Mack Stadium; Thomas was released after the game and proceeded to tell the Philly sports media his side of the story. The club forbade Allen to speak publicly about it; from that moment on, many fans sided with the veteran first baseman. They turned on the 1964 National Rookie of the Year with loud boos, racial slurs, hate mail, vandalism of his home, and projectiles thrown from the stands. While playing under an avalanche of abuse for the next four seasons, Allen repeatedly begged the Phils to trade him. After the 1969 season, the team finally granted his request and shipped him to the St. Louis Cardinals.

Frank Thomas was out of baseball by 1967. In a way, it's unfortunate that his brawl with Allen is the only thing many people remember about him. Thomas put up some good numbers for an extended period. But he brought the perception on himself; even if Allen had overreacted, Thomas didn't need to club the young third baseman with his bat. Any negativity surrounding his diamond legacy was of his own doing. Frank Thomas gets no sympathy here.

1954 Sid Gordon *(Pittsburgh Pirates)*. Nominated five times for AL MVP during his career, the 36-year-old Gordon was a valuable member of manager Haney's ensemble in 1954. He could plug Gordon into any outfield spot or use him at third when the need arose. The 5'10", 185-pound Brooklyn, New York native led the team in hitting with a .306 AVG, registered a lofty .405 OBP, and swatted 12 home runs.

1954 Dick Littlefield *(Pittsburgh Pirates)*. The Pirates didn't have a very good pitching staff in 1954. Littlefield was OK with a 10-11 record and 3.60 ERA but didn't have pinpoint control (85 walks over 155 innings pitched). Honorable Mention.

1955 Mickey Vernon *(Washington Senators 53-101)*. One of the all-time greats. Winner of two batting titles, Vernon made the AL All-Star team seven times. Along with being a fine hitter, he was probably the best fielding first baseman in the Junior Circuit between 1946-1956. His average and OBP in 1955 were award-worthy .301 and .384. In addition, he clubbed 14 home runs and knocked in 85 teammates.

1955 Pete Runnels *(Washington Senators)*. Another member of the Senators that won a couple of batting crowns during his career, Runnels, was a singles hitter and a darn good one. He batted .284 with a .353 OBP while putting in time at second, third, and left field.

1955 Eddie Yost *(Washington Senators)*. The man had a real "camera eye" when at the plate, with a talent for laying off bad pitches. His average was only .243, BUT his OBP was an excellent .407, thanks to 95 walks combined with his hit total. 1955 was the only year between 1948 and 1959 that Yost *did not* lead AL third basemen in putouts. He also led the league twice in errors committed at the hot corner but was a sturdy player who was in the line-up almost every day and handled many chances.

1955 Roy Sievers *(Washington Senators)*. His INBB award-winning line: .271AVG, .364 OBP, 25 HR, 8 triples, and 106 RBI. Sievers won the AL "Rookie-of-Year Award" in 1949 but then seemed to lose his baseball mojo between 1950 and 1952. After splitting time between the majors and minors for those three seasons, Sievers rediscovered the stroke he had during his first season. For the next 11 seasons, he was one of baseball's most consistent power hitters.

1955 Carlos Paula *(Washington Senators)*. For such an awful record, The Senators had some gentlemen who could hit. Born in Cuba, the outfielder spent only three years in the USA big leagues. He played his best ball in America in 1955 when he appeared in 115 games and hit .299. Paula also put in seven years in the minor leagues, hitting .300, .309 (twice), .315, and .334 during his best seasons. He hung up the spikes after hitting .334 as a member of the Mexico City Tigers in 1960.

1955 Pedro Ramos *(Washington Senators)*. The rookie season stats weren't too bad for Ramos (five wins, 3.88 ERA, 1.231 WHIP). His five saves led the team, and as a spot starter, "Pete" completed three games. One of the few decent pitchers at manager Chuck Dressen's disposal during another train wreck of a season for Washington.

1956 Vic Power *(Kansas City A's 52-102)*. The move to the Midwest didn't do anything to help the A's won-lost record, but there were some interesting players on their roster. First baseman Power was a hot dog with occasional on-the-field theatrics, but he backed up the show with a .309 average, 77 runs scored, and 63 RBI. He was an outstanding fielder (.993), too.

1956 Hector Lopez *(Kansas City A's)*. Used mainly as a third sacker, Lopez contributed 18 home runs and 69 RBI to the A's attack but was a brutal fielder (26 errors). He also put time in at second, short, and the outfield and didn't fare any better at those positions with the glove. He might have won an INBB, but his glove work precludes the Committee from bestowing that honor on the man from Colon, Panama. However, his work with the stick earns Lopez an Honorable Mention.

Sort of Random Trivia: Yankee Don Larsen's perfect game in the 1956 World Series was one for ages. However, it appears that his marriage was less than perfect. Larsen's wife divorced him on the day he mowed down 27 straight Brooklyn Dodgers.

1956 Gus Zernial *(Kansas City A's)*. The one-time AL home run and RBI champ (1951) was relieved when the team moved to Kansas City. For some reason, fans in Philadelphia didn't appreciate his seasons of 29, 30, 33, and 42 home runs and several 100 plus RBI campaigns and booed him mercilessly. As a platoon player in 1956, Zernial delivered 16 home runs and 44 RBI in 109 games. Honorable Mention. A low .224 BA and .315 OBP kept "Ozark Ike" from winning the *big* award.

One thumb-up is better than none, isn't it?

1956 Wally Burnette *(Kansas City A's)*. While toiling in the Yankee minor league system, Burnette's posted seasons of 14, 15, and 21 wins. Traded to KC in July of 1956 for another pitcher, Tommy Lasorda, Burnette acquitted himself quite well during his rookie season. The 27-year-old won 6 games, posted an effective 2.89 ERA and a nice 1.269 WHIP. It would be his best season in the big leagues, pitching for Kansas City through the 1958 campaign.

1956 Tom Gorman *(Kansas City A's)*. Honorable Mention. In 52 games as a reliever and occasional starter, the 31-year-old right-hander was the winning hurler in nine games. His ERA and WHIP were satisfactory (3.83, 1.377), but he served up 23 home runs over 171 innings.

1957 No 100-loss teams, but the Senators came darn close, dropping 99 contests. We need to have standards, so no awards or honorable mentions are bestowed.

1958 Well, Fredo, what do you know? Once again, we find ourselves with no 100-loss duds.

1959 Both leagues were fairly competitive at the end of the decade. In 1959, both cellar dwellers (Phillies, Senators) "only" lost 90 and 91 games. Both clubs were bad, but they weren't historically rotten like the other teams we've discussed in this chapter.

Ned Garver managed to win 20 games on a Browns team that lost 102 games in 1951. (Courtesy Detroit Free Press Archives)

The Big Bopper in the Bucs' line-up in the early 1950s: Ralph Kiner. (Courtesy Bowman Gum)

Pedro Ramos earns an INBB for his mound work as a Rookie in 1955. (Courtesy Jay Publishing)

Baseball's version of "Father Time," 46-year-old Satchel Paige, led the 1954 Browns in saves. (Courtesy Acme Newspictures)

Flashy Vic Power delivered with the bat and the glove for the Kansas City Athletics in 1958. (Courtesy Cleveland Press)

The Polo Grounds: Home to the 1951 and 1954 NL pennant-winning New York Giants. (Courtesy *The Sporting News*)

Roy Campanella of the Dodgers was probably the best catcher in the National League in the 1950s. (Courtesy Bowman Gum)

The pipeline of talented Cuban players going to the USA was shut-off when this fellow took power on the island nation in 1959. (Courtesy Cuban government archives)

June 1950: U.N. forces, led by the United States, intervened in response to a North Korean invasion of their neighbor to the south. (U.S. Marine Corps photo)

The 1960s

I Want to Hold Your Hand

Some important stuff that happened in the 1960s:

- The first televised U.S. Presidential debate took place in Chicago. The September 1960 match-up pitted Democrat John F. Kennedy against Republican Richard M. Nixon.

- On January 21, 1961, John Kennedy is sworn in as the 35th President of the United States. The 43-year-old Kennedy was the youngest and the first Roman Catholic to become president.

- Construction on the one-hundred-mile wall to separate East Germany from West Germany began on August 13, 1961. The Communist government in the East built it to keep its citizens from fleeing to the West.

- In October 1962, the world breathed a sigh of relief after Russia agreed to withdraw offensive nuclear missiles from Cuba. The U.S. had blockaded the island nation, a move that raised the possibility of an all-out nuclear war between the superpowers.

- With over 200,000 in attendance, Dr. Martin Luther King, Jr. delivered his famous "I Have A Dream" speech in front of the Lincoln Memorial at the U.S. capitol. The date was August 28, 1963.

- President Kennedy was shot to death while riding in a motorcade on November 22, 1963, in Dallas, Texas. Two days later, the accused assassin, Lee Harvey Oswald, was shot and killed while in the custody of the Dallas police department.

- A cultural earthquake occurs when The Beatles appeared on *The Ed Sullivan Show* for the first time on February 9, 1964. Millions of

Americans watched the quartet with "long hair" introduce their new and innovative style of Rock and Roll.

• North Vietnamese torpedo boats allegedly attacked the U.S.S. *Maddox* in the Gulf of Tonkin on April 4, 1964, sparking a major U.S. military response that would become the Vietnam War. Almost 60,000 American service people will be killed and about 150,000 wounded before the conflict ended in 1975.

• Assassins' bullets felled civil rights leader Dr. Martin Luther King, Jr and Democratic presidential candidate Robert F. Kennedy within two months of each other in 1968. (April, June).

• In July 1969, the United States successfully landed a manned spacecraft on the Moon. The first man to set foot on the Moon's surface, Neil Armstrong, uttered the famous phrase, "That's one small step for man, one giant leap for mankind."

Some important stuff that happened in Major League Baseball in the 1960s:

• An exciting 1960 World Series ended with a dramatic home run by second baseman Bill Mazeroski. The blast propelled the Pittsburgh Pirates over the New York Yankees to capture baseball's World Championship.

• The American League expanded from eight to ten teams. The new clubs are the Los Angeles Angels and the (new) Washington Senators. To accommodate the added teams, the league schedule is expanded from 154 to 162 games.

• Yankees outfielder Roger Maris slammed a record-breaking 61st home run on October 1, 1961. The blast eclipsed the previous record of 60 homers in a season set by Babe Ruth in 1927.

• The National League added two new teams, the Houston Astros and the New York Mets, for the 1962 campaign. The schedule is expanded from 154 games to 162 games.

• St. Louis Cardinals great Stan Musial retired after the 1963 season. Musial finished with a lifetime average of .331 and a then all-time major league record of 3,360 career hits.

- June 21, 1964. Using only 90 pitches, Jim Bunning of the Phillies hurled the 7th perfect game in major league history when he shut out the New York Mets 6-0.

- In 1966, star pitchers Sandy Koufax and Don Drysdale staged a joint hold-out, demanding 167,000 dollars per player for three seasons. After negotiation, the Dodgers agreed to pay Koufax 125,000 and Drysdale 110,000 dollars per season.

- Carl Yastrzemski of the Boston Red Sox won the 1968 American League batting title with a .301 average. It was the lowest average ever to win the batting crown.

- Both leagues decided to expand to 12 teams for the 1969 season. The American League add clubs in Seattle and Kansas City. The National League placed teams in Montreal and San Diego.

- Once the laughing-stock of baseball, the New York Mets caught fire in the 2nd half of the 1969 season to win the National League pennant. They then proceeded to shock the heavily favored Baltimore Orioles in the World Series four games to one.

◆ ◆ ◆

Summers were real bummers for the teams these hearty souls played for in the 1960s. Here are the winners of the esteemed "I Am Not A Baseball Bozo Award" for that decade:

1960 What a way to get started—no awards for the first year of the decade. Never fear. It only gets better (worse?) from here on in!

1961 Norm Siebern (*Kansas City Athletics 61-101*). The veteran first baseman clubbed 18 home runs, slashed 32 doubles, and drove in 98 runs while batting a fine .296. Impressive numbers for a team that finished in-or-near-the-bottom in league offensive categories.

1961 Jerry Lumpe (*Kansas City Athletics*). Not only did Lumpe shine at the plate (.293 AVG, 29 doubles, 9 triples), he helped the A's in the field. He finished 3rd among AL second basemen with a .979 fielding percentage.

Siebern and Lumpe were the only positional players on the As to win an INBB in 1961, but third sacker Wayne Causey deserves a little recognition.

His .276 AVG and 49 RBIs in 312 at-bats netted him an Honorable Mention. As a reminder, instead of one of those fancy gold-plated trophies that all INBB winners receive, Honorable Mentions get a hearty virtual pat-on-the-back.

1961 Jim Archer (*Kansas City Athletics*). To say the least, the As had pitching problems in 1961. Overall, they finished 10th (out of 10 teams) in ERA (4.74), hits allowed (1519), and runs allowed (863). They managed ninth-place finishes in strikeouts (703) and complete games (32). Mr. Archer rose above all this lousiness with a good 3.20 ERA, and 1.286 WHIP over 205 innings pitched.

With 11 wins, Archer's mound mate Norm Bass might have won an INBB or been recognized with an Honorable Mention had his ERA and WHIP been better (4.69, 1.441).

1961 Gene Green (*Washington Senators 61-101*). The line for the 29-year-old from Los Angeles (.280 AVG, 18 HR, 62 RBI, .341 OBP). INBB.

1961 Gene Woodling (*Washington Senators*). The one-time Yankee star was even better than Green with a .313 AVG and .403 OBP.

1961 Danny O'Connell (Washington Senators). The 32-year-old veteran infielder earned one of them award thingies for his work during the Senators' woe-begone season. His .260 batting mark was sixteen points higher than the club's overall average (.244). O'Connell's .361 OBP was good, and his 30 doubles led the team. To top it off, he finished 2nd on the Senators in steals with 15.

Sort of Random Trivia: Cuban revolutionary dictator Fidel Castro attended the University of Havana and reportedly starred on the school's baseball team. (I wonder if his star status was forged *before* or *after* his rise to power.)

1961 Dale Long (*Washington Senators*). It's an Honorable Mention for Long. His 17 home runs and 49 RBI in 377 at-bats were respectable, but that OBP (.317) did nothing to help his cause.

1961 Bennie Daniels (*Washington Senators*). The Senators' main problem in 1961 was not pitching. The staff finished in the middle of the pack in most of the major AL overall categories, and a couple of their hurlers had good years. Daniels posted a winning record (12-11) with a decent 3.44 ERA. Over 212 innings of work, he only allowed 184 hits and just 14 home runs.

1961 Dick Donovan (*Washington Senators*) pitched 168 innings and logged an impressive 2.44 ERA and a tiny 1.026 WHIP.

1961 Joe McClain (*Washington Senators*). His ERA was 3.69, and the man posted a good 1.269 WHIP and only walked 48 in 212 innings of work. But he lost 18 games and surrendered 22 dingers. Borderline guy—what should the Committee do? Hmmm.

Wait. I'm getting a text.

It says that the Committee is feeling generous today and awards Mc-Clain an INBB.

It also says that I need to return the hedge clippers I borrowed from Mr. Myself a year ago.

C'mon, guys, it hasn't been *that* long.

I should mention the fact that the Senators franchise of 1961 was not the Senators of 1960. The Washington team of 1960 moved to Minneapolis-St. Paul for the 1961 campaign and became the Twins. The Senators of 1961 were brand new.

1961 Tony Gonzalez (*Philadelphia Phillies 47-107*). The 1961 Phillies were a dumpster fire of epic proportions, a season that included a losing streak of 23 straight games. However, there were some bright spots for the Phils. One was outfielder Tony Gonzalez. At bat, the native Cuban hit .277 for a club that collectively hit .243. His OBP was more-than-adequate (.358), plus he slammed 12 home runs and stole 15 bases. In the field, Gonzalez was excellent, committing only 4 errors over 126 games. I once met Tony at a card show; he was very friendly and seemed like a genuinely nice man.

1961 Johnny Callison (*Philadelphia Phillies*). The team's young right fielder showed a lot of promise with a .266 average and .363 OBP. He banged 11 triples and led the team in runs scored with 77. Over the next few seasons, Callison would blossom into one of the most-feared power hitters in the National League.

1961 Don Demeter (*Philadelphia Phillies*). Acquired during the season from the Dodgers, utility man Don Demeter smacked 20 home runs and plated 68 teammates over 382 at-bats. Demeter would continue being a productive member of Philly's red pinstripes over the next two seasons before being traded to the Tigers for a pitcher named Bunning.

1961 Art Mahaffey (*Philadelphia Phillies*). Manager Gene Mauch's #1 fan (not!) gets an INBB for his work in 1961. In 219 innings pitched, he won 11, whiffed 158, and put up a respectable 1.254 WHIP. He also lost 19 games and served up 27 long balls, but those other numbers carry him over the line.

1961 Jack Baldschun (*Philadelphia Phillies*). You might think that no hurler deserves positive recognition on a team that finished dead last in the NL in ERA, earned runs, and complete games plus next-to-last in hits allowed (at least *I* might). But the Phillies had another guy who did sort of OK despite the statistical carnage around him, and that fella was Baldschun. The man with a wicked screwball went 5-3 with a 3.88 ERA. His hits-per-innings pitched wasn't too bad (100/90), as was his 1.254 WHIP.

Sort of Random Trivia: When Roger Maris slammed a then-record-breaking 61 home runs in 1961, he drew zero (0) intentional walks. The fact that slugger Mickey Mantle (54 home runs himself) batted next in the batting order might have helped a little.

1962 Ernie Banks (*Chicago Cubs 59-103*). "Mr. Cub" launched 37 home runs and to go along with 104 RBI.

1962 Billy Williams (*Chicago Cubs*). Along with being an offensive powerhouse (.298 AVG, 22 HR, 91 RBI, .369 OBP), the future Hall-of-Famer was also one of the best fielding left fielders in all of baseball. Possessor of a powerful arm, he nailed 17 base runners trying to advance on the base paths in 1962.

1962 George Altman (*Chicago Cubs*). The big guy didn't let his club's lack of success get him down. Altman posted the highest batting average on the Cubs (.318), hit 22 homers, drove in 74, and slugged a lofty .511. For his work, the outfielder earned a spot on the NL All-Star team AND the outrageously prestigious INBB.

1962 Don Elston (*Chicago Cubs*). As the closer, his 2.44 ERA, a WHIP of 1.342, and paltry eight saves gained Elston an INBB by the slimmest of margins.

1962 Barney Shultz (*Chicago Cubs*). Shultz was probably the best hurler on a mediocre Cubs staff, which isn't saying much. His 3.82 ERA was high, but his 1.146 WHIP was excellent. A long-of-tooth veteran at age 35, the right-hander proved he could still "bring it" by fanning 58 over 73 innings.

1962 Bob Buhl (*Chicago Cubs*). An Honorable Mention went to the veteran pitcher. Buhl was the club's top winner (12) and registered an ERA of 3.69 but walked almost 100 batters over 34 games and served up 23 gopher balls. His 1.406 WHIP was subpar.

1962 Felix Mantilla (*New York Mets 40-120*). Wacky and woeful, the Mets captured the hearts of fans all over the country despite their pronounced lack of success on the field. As that initial campaign wore on, Mets' skipper Casey Stengel said, "The only thing worse than a Mets game is a Mets doubleheader."

As bad as they were, the club had some decent players. Three men who saw significant playing time during that historically terrible season deserve an INBB for their work. Third baseman Felix Mantilla netted one for batting .275, hitting 11 home runs and driving in 59 runs.

1962 Frank Thomas (*New York Mets*). While his team was losing game-after-game, the power-hitting first baseman kept focused and finished the season with 34 home runs and 94 runs-batted-in.

1962 Richie Ashburn (*New York Mets*). The last season for the Hall of Fame outfielder was a good one. Over 373 at-bats, the man from Tilden, Nebraska, registered a .306 BA and .424 OBP. Never a power hitter, Ashburn smacked a career-high seven long balls. In 1963, Richie began a career as a broadcaster for the Philadelphia Phillies and, for the next 35 years, would often share humorous stories on-air about the 1962 Mets team.

1962 Chuck Hinton (*Washington Senators 60-101*). It was a career year for the outfielder/infielder. Playing in 151 games, his line was: .310 AVG, .361 OBP, 17 HR, 75 RBI, 28 SB. Sure-handed with the glove, Hinton committed only 3 errors over 1138 innings.

1962 Harry Bright (*Washington Senators*). The 32-year-old spent most of the season as the team's starting first baseman but also put in a few innings behind the plate and at third base. Bright launched 17 home runs to tie Chuck Hinton for the team lead. His batting average was half-decent (.273), and his 67 RBI were good for 2nd place on the Senators. His stats are noteworthy on a club that finished dead last in runs scored (out of 10 teams) and 9th in OBP and SLG.

1962 Bob Johnson (*Washington Senators*). A .288 AVG and .334 OBP plus power numbers of 20 doubles, 2 triples, and 12 home runs were just good enough for the "I Am Not a Baseball Bozo" Award.

1962 Dave Stenhouse (*Washington Senators*). Manager Mickey Vernon's pitching staff wasn't too bad. Even though they registered the 7th highest ERA in the AL, his hurlers ranked 4th in hits allowed and 5th in home runs surrendered and shutouts. Staff ace Dave Stenhouse pitched 197 innings, struck out 147, and logged a good 3.62 ERA. Unfortunately, injury problems limited his effectiveness over the next two seasons, and by 1965, Stenhouse found himself in the minors. After three unsuccessful years trying to return to the big leagues, the two-time AL All-Star retired following the 1967 season.

1962 Tom Cheney (*Washington Senators*). The 27-year-old righthander posted a 3.17 ERA, excellent hits per inning pitched ratio of 173/134, and a whiff total of 147.

1962 Claude Osteen (*Washington Senators*). Osteen's first year as a member of a starting rotation. Although his overall record of 8-13 wasn't great, an ERA of 3.65 and WHIP of 1.244 ranked above most of his mound mates.

1963 Duke Snider (*New York Mets 51-111*). On a team that collectively hit .215 and reached base at a minuscule .285 percentage, Snider's .243 AVG and .345 OBP look good. In addition, he slammed 14 home runs in 354 at-bats to finish second on the team in circuit clouts.

Hey, I think that's the first time I've used the phrase "circuit clouts" in this book. As a matter of fact, I'm pretty sure I've never used it before in any of my baseball articles or tomes. It's a catchy phrase, too. I need to use it again sometime.

1963 Frank Thomas (*New York Mets*). His performance in 1963 didn't come close to matching that of 1962 (34 circuit clouts, 94 RBI) but were still worthy of INBB (15 HR, 60 RBI).

1963 Ron Hunt (*New York Mets*). Clear winner of an INBB with a .272 AVG, .334 OBP, 10 HR, and 28 stolen bases. A first-year player in 1963, Hunt finished 2nd behind Pete Rose in NL Rookie of the Year voting.

1963 Carl Wiley (*New York Mets*). Winner of nine games, Wiley posted a good 3.10 ERA and struck out 101 batters over 183 innings while allowing just 149 hits.

1963 Al Jackson (*New York Mets*). Mr. Jackson qualifies for an Honorable Mention, thanks to leading the staff with 13 wins and 11 complete games. However, a high 3.96 ERA and 1.414 WHIP plus 25 home runs surrendered work against an outright INBB.

1963 Larry Bearnarth (*New York Mets*). Casey's "closer" in 1963, the rookie finished 34 games and garnered a satisfactory 3.42 ERA. His team-leading four (count 'em-*four*) saves says a lot about the ineptitude of the Mets during their last season at the Polo Grounds.

1963 Chuck Hinton (*Washington Senators 56-106*). A second INBB for Hinton. His .269 average was 22 points better than the AL average (.247), and his OBP (.340) was considerably higher than the rest of the league (.312). Along with 15 circuit clouts and 55 RBI, Hinton wiped 25 bases.

1963 Don Lock (*Washington Senators*). Lock emerged as a "power guy" in 1963 with 27 circuit clouts and 82 RBI. Even though the outfielder fanned a lot (152), he was on base plenty with a.338 OBP, thanks largely to 72 walks. With the glove, Lock was outstanding. He led the AL in outfield putouts (377) and assists (19) and only committed 8 errors in 146 games.

Wait. I'm getting another text from the Committee.

It says, "Knock off the use of the phrase "circuit clouts." It's already old, and you're going to lose readers, and it's not that funny."

To which I reply, who's joking?

Well, I guess I better listen to their advice. But I just might use "circuit clouts" again in the future.

1963 Jim King (*Washington Senators*). The Senators had a quality outfield in 1963. Along with INBB winners Hinton and Lock, right fielder Jim King earned an Honorable Mention. The man from Arkansas smashed 24 HR and plated 62 runs; a .231 BA and .300 OBP prevented him from getting an INBB. Members of the "Jim King Fan Club" will probably be disappointed, but hey, we need to have standards, don't we?

1963 Claude Osteen (*Washington Senators*). This one is probably going to hack a few people off—Osteen gets an Honorable Mention instead of an INBB for his mound work in 1963. Yeah, he led the club in wins (9) and posted a worthy 3.35 ERA, but over 212 innings, he surrendered 222 hits, including 23 home runs. The best was yet to come; over the next 16 years, Osteen would go on to have two 20-win seasons and 7 seasons with victory totals of 14 or more.

1964 Jim Gentile (*Kansas City A's 57-105*). The 1960s was not a great decade for the A's. Habitually buried in the AL second division, one might think it was extremely hard to root for Charlie Finley's boys. But fans were blessed with a few good performances from men who wore the A's uniform. One such performance was Jim Gentile's in 1964 (28 HR, 71 RBI, .372 OBP).

1964 Rocky Colavito (*Kansas City A's*). Another player that helped keep Kansas City fans from jumping off bridges or from the top of tall buildings was Mr. Colavito. In 1964, "The Rock" belted 34 HR, compiled 102 RBI, and slugged at .507 clip. A lot of people around baseball were impressed;

Colavito was named to the AL All-Star team and received a few votes for league MVP.

1964 Wayne Causey (*Kansas City A's*). Mainly a shortstop, Causey also logged innings at second and third base. A good fielder, the former "Bonus Baby" finished 4th in putouts (266) and range factor (4.94). Not just a glove man, Causey hit .281, ripped 31 doubles, and reached base a league-best 265 times. . He, too, received a handful of votes for AL MVP.

1964 Ed Charles (*Kansas City A's*). The man nicknamed "EZ" earned an INBB with a line that included 16 HR, 63 RBI, and 25 doubles.

1964 Wes Stock (*Kansas City A's*). Stock treated beleaguered A's fans to some good pitching. The entire staff finished dead last (out of 10 teams) in ERA, complete games, hits, earned runs, hits, walks, and home runs allowed. Stock was wonderful with a 6-3 record, 1.94 ERA, fanned 101, and allowed only 69 hits in 91 innings pitched.

1964 Dick Green and John Wyatt (*Kansas City A's*). Why did I group an infielder and pitcher together? Two reasons:

1. Both are Honorable Mention recipients.
2. I felt like it.

Second baseman Dick Green hit .264 on a team that collectively hit .239. He also hit 11 HR, not a bad number of dingers for a middle infielder. By now, you probably realize the INBB panel's obsession with OBP and Green's was a mediocre .311. An outstanding fielder; his .990 was #2 among regular AL second sackers.

The plusses for Green's teammate John Wyatt include 20 saves and a league-leading 81 appearances. The negatives are a) a not-so "lights-out" 3.59 ERA and b) a whopping 23 home runs surrendered.

1964 Joseph O'Neal Christopher (*New York Mets 53-109*). I think his full name looks and sounds groovy, so I decided it to print it here. The gent from the Virgin Islands was outstanding in 1964 (.300 AVG, .360 OBP, 16 HR, 76 RBI). Furthermore, he scored 78 runs, walked 83 times, and ranked third among NL right fielders in fielding percentage (.979). He may have been the best player on the Mets that season.

1964 Ron Hunt (*New York Mets*). For his efforts, the second baseman was named to the NL All-Star squad and received a smattering of support for league MVP. His .303 AVG was good, and a .357 OBP was helped by 11 hit-by-pitches. Hunt was a tough, gritty performer who didn't give an inch and always gave 110%.

(Don't you just love baseball clichés?)

1964 Charlie Smith (*New York Mets*). Honorable Mention. The infielder launched 20 HR and compiled 58 RBI. The rest of his offensive contribution was negligible (.239 AVG, .275 OBP, 102 Ks), and he was a brutal fielder (32 errors).

1964 Jesse Gonder (*New York Mets*). Honorable Mention. His line: .270 AVG, 7 HR, 374 plate appearances.

1964 Galen Cisco (*New York Mets*). INBB. Even though he lost 19 games, his overall stats were first-rate (3.62 ERA, 1.231 WHIP, 54 walks in 192 innings pitched). After his playing days, Cisco was a pitching coach for several teams over 26 seasons.

1964 Tracey Stallard (*New York Mets*). Yet another Honorable Mention for one of Stengel's minions. Stallard posted a 3.79 ERA, 11 complete games, and a 1.267 WHIP. He did finish 2nd on the team in wins (10) but lost more games than anyone else in the National League (20).

1964 Don Lock (*Washington Senators 62-100*). Another horrendous season for Senators, version 2.0. Centerfielder Don Lock whiffed a lot (137) but was productive at the plate (28 HR, 80 RBI). An excellent fielder with a rifle arm, he led all AL outfielders in assists (19).

1964 Chuck Hinton (*Washington Senators*). Yet another INBB award for the pride of Rocky Mount, North Carolina.

How many is that now?

Two? Three?

I forget.

What matters is the man's consistent performance despite his club's difficulties. In 1964, he hit .274 on a team that finished dead last in batting average (.231). His OBP was a solid (.346), he socked 11 HR, ripped seven triples, and finished 5th in the league in stolen bases with 17. Not a bad season, don't you think?

1964 Jim King (*Washington Senators*). King earned an INBB but by the slimmest of margins. He did slam 18 HR and drive in 56 RBI in just 415 at-bats. BUT his batting average and slugging percentage weren't overly impressive (.241, .412). However, his OBP (.338) was high enough to help push him into INBB territory.

1964 Bill Skowron (*Washington Senators*). Some of his numbers in just 278 plate appearances were good (.271 AVG, 13 HR, 41 RB), but his OBP was terrible (.306). Honorable Mention.

1964 Steve Ridizik (*Washington Senators*). The Senators pitching staff finished at or near the bottom statistically in most categories. Luckily for the fans in Washington, some bright spots put in innings for Manager Hodges. Steve Ridizik was one (2.89 ERA, 1.134 WHIP over 112 innings pitched). Other "higher" achievers included Claude Osteen (15-13, 3.33 ERA, 1.245 WHIP), Bennie Daniels (8-10, 3.70 ERA, 1.294 WHIP), and closer Ron Cline (10-7, 2.32 ERA, 1.254 WHIP, 14 saves).

Kudos to these men; they persevered and won an INBB!

1965 Lee Thomas (*Boston Red Sox 62-100*). It was a strange season in Beantown. The club lost many games, but several players had good seasons, giving Red Sox loyalists something to get excited about. First baseman Lee Thomas propelled 22 HR, drove in 75, while batting .271 with a .361 OBP.

1965 Felix Mantilla (*Boston Red Sox*). INBB #2 for the veteran infielder. His line: .275 AVG, .374 OBP, 18 HR, 92 RBI. Mantilla made the All-Star team and received a few MVP votes.

1965 Carl Yastrzemski (*Boston Red Sox*). Nagging injuries kept him out of the line-up from time to time, but Number 8 still managed a .312 average, .395 OBP, 20 homers, and 45 doubles in 133 games. A master of dealing with the Green Monster in left, Yaz committed just 3 errors and recorded 11 assists.

1965 Tony Conigliaro (*Boston Red Sox*). The 20-year-old, 2nd-year-man blasted 32 home runs and slugged at a terrific .512 clip. His OBP was .338. Do I need to say anything else?

1965 Lenny Green (Boston Red Sox). Lenny batted .276 with a .361 OBP and scored 69 runs over 427 plate appearances.

1965 Earl Wilson (*Boston Red Sox*). His era was high (3.98), but he did win 13 games, strike out 164 over 231 innings, and finished with a 1.292 WHIP.

1965 Dick Radatz (*Boston Red Sox*). Honorable Mention for "The Monster." Allowing that walk-off home run to Johnny Callison in the 1964 All-Star Game seemed to shake his confidence and started a downward spiral in the career of the once overpowering reliever. Radatz did whiff 121 batters in 124 innings and saved 22 games in 1965, but his ERA (3.91) was way too elevated for a closer. Over the next four seasons, his ERAs would balloon from 4.64 to 6.56, and by 1970 he would be out of the major leagues.

1965 Bill Monbouquette (*Boston Red Sox*). Honorable Mention. He won ten games with a 3.70 ERA and 1.220 WHIP. But a whopping 32 home runs yielded for an average of 1.3 dingers per game prevents William M. from capturing an INBB outright.

1965 Dick Duliba (*Boston Red Sox*). Duliba's line: 4-2, 3.74 ERA, 1.263 WHIP. His stats are similar to Monbouquette's, BUT he permitted under one home run for every nine innings he pitched (.08).

1965 Bert Campaneris (*Kansas City A's 59-103*). Hit for a decent average (.270) and stole a bunch of bases (51). His OBP of .326 wasn't great; you'd like the lead-off guy to get on base a bit more often. Still, he slashed 12 triples and led the AL in being HBP with nine. Campy wasn't great with the glove, finishing 2nd in the league in errors at shortstop with 30. He would go on to lead the Junior circuit in miscues at short three times over his career. Despite a couple of weaknesses, Campaneris qualifies for an INBB.

1965 Ken Harrelson (*Kansas City A's*). It was another rough year for the A's, but first baseman Ken Harrelson managed to hit 23 HR and record 66 RBI. His batting average was mediocre (.238), but his OBP was passable (.329), and he committed the second-lowest number of errors at first in the league (9).

1965 Jack Acker (*Kansas City A's*). With 51 innings pitched, reliever Jack Acker barely qualified for the award. His 3.16 ERA and 1.227 WHIP sparkled like a star on a clear night on a staff that collectively registered a 4.24 ERA and 1.337 WHIP. Acker would become one of the best relievers in the AL for the next several seasons.

1965 Johnny Lewis (*New York Mets 50-112*). Johnny *who*? Career year (of sorts) for this long-forgotten member of the traveling loss machine known as the Mets in the mid-1960s. With an eventual lifetime batting average of .227, Lewis "exploded" for a .245 mark and clobbered 15 home runs in pitcher-friendly Shea Stadium. In the context of an overall team batting average of .221, his .245 is noticeable, although not exactly deserving of being given the keys to the city. Honorable Mention.

1965 Frank Lary (*New York Mets*). The man from Tuscaloosa, Alabama, wrapped up a good 12-year career (124 wins, 3.49 ERA) in 1965.

Did you know that in Alabama, the tusks are looser? It's true!

If you don't believe me, just ask Captain Spaulding!

Hooray, hooray, hooray!

(For you younger readers, the preceding was a reference to an old movie. If you'd like to know what the heck "Captain Spaulding" is about, I suggest searching for "Groucho Marx." I need to throw stuff like this in to keep the Baby Boomers happy.)

Before being traded later in the season to the White Sox, Lary put up a .298 ERA and 1.16 WHIP over 14 games (seven as a starter). Things didn't go as well as a member of the Pale Hose, and Lary decided to hang 'em up at season's end. Honorable Mention.

1965 Gordie Richardson (*New York Mets*). Gordie came over with Lewis in a trade with the Cardinals before the season. He went 2-2 with a 3.78 ERA and 1.089 WHIP and finished second on the Mets in saves. Honorable Mention.

1965 Jack Fisher (*New York Mets*). He also gets an Honorable Mention. Poor Guy. His atrocious record (8-24) was mainly attributable to the nightmare squad that backed him up (last in the league in hitting, near the bottom in fielding percentage and errors committed). Through the carnage, "Fat Jack" sported a 1.261 WHIP and fanned 116 in 254 innings pitched.

1966 Glen Beckert (*Chicago Cubs 59-103*). In one of my earlier books, I wrote a compelling essay on the paradox of a talented 1966 Cubs team finishing dead last. The piece should have won an award or two; I was hurt and disappointed for a while, but I'm over it now.

Manager Leo Durocher had some potent weapons in his arsenal. One was second sacker Glen Beckert who hit .287 and drove in 59 runs, outstanding figures for a top-of-the-lineup type of guy.

1966 Ron Santo (*Chicago Cubs*). Another big stick for The Lip was Santo (.312 AVG, .412 OBP, 30 HR, 94 RBI). That OBP led the NL, and the man also won the Gold Glove for his work at third base. Santo passed away in 2010, two years before he was elected to the Hall-of-Fame.

1966 Billy Williams (*Chicago Cubs*). Another eventual Cooperstown inductee, "Sweet Swinging" Billy, pounded 29 homers, knocked in 91, and scored 100. A durable player, he played in all 162 games and only committed 8 errors in the outfield.

1966 Adolfo Phillips (*Chicago Cubs*). Came over from the Phillies in the Fergie Jenkins deal and batted .262 with 16 HR and a .348 OBP.

1966 Ken Holtzman (*Chicago Cubs*). Durocher's major problem in 1966 was a lack of quality pitching. The Cubbies were the worst in the league in ERA, hits allowed, runs allowed, and home runs surrendered. Despite this, two gentlemen did all right for Leo. Holtzman led the staff with 11 wins, whiffed 171 in 221 innings pitched, and finished with an excellent 1.181 WHIP. Thanks largely to 27 long balls served up, his ERA was elevated (3.79), but that kind of thing often happens to a pitcher who makes half of his starts in the windy confines of Wrigley Field.

1966 Fergie Jenkins (*Chicago Cubs*). I'm not going to harp on how bad a trade this was for the Phillies. Or at least, *not much*. The Phils thought veterans Larry Jackson and Bob Buhl were what they needed to capture the pennant that had evaded them since1964. Jackson did OK but Buhl stunk. Jenkins developed into one of the best hurlers in the major leagues and eventually landed in the Hall of Fame in 1991. Over 182 innings pitched in 1966, Fergie's stats included a 3.31 ERA, 1.088 WHIP, and 148 K.

1967 Tommy Davis (*New York Mets 61-101*). His line: .302 average, 16 home runs, 32 doubles, and 73 RBI. As a unit, the Mets managed a paltry .238 AVG and horrible .288 OBP.

1967 Ron Swoboda (*New York Mets*). Swoboda's line was close to what would eventually be considered a typical season during his 9-year career:

1967 (.281 AVG, .340 OBP, 13 HR, 17 doubles, 3 triples, 53 RBI)
Career (.242 AVG, .324 OBP, 13 HR, 15 doubles, 4 triples, 60 RBI)

Besides Davis, no one else on the Mets had a year nearly as good as the native Baltimorean.

Got that, Hon?

1967 Tom Seaver (*New York Mets*). Tom "Terrific" was NL Rookie of the Year in 1967 (16 wins, 2.76 ERA, 1.203 WHIP, 170 K in 251 innings pitched).

1967 Ron Taylor (*New York Mets*). The bullpen did surprisingly well in 1967, considering Mets pitching finished 8th overall in team ERA and earned runs and 9th in home runs and walks allowed. Taylor led the team in saves (8) and recorded a 2.34 ERA and a 1.137 WHIP.

1967 Dick Selma (*New York Mets*). The fireballing righty took home an INBB thanks to a 2.77 ERA, 1.316 WHIP, 55 K, and only 3 homers served up in 81 innings pitched.

1967 Don Shaw (*New York Mets*). With 51 innings of work, Shaw squeaked over the qualification line. He gets an INBB for striking out 44 batters, posting a 2.98 ERA and 1.227 WHIP.

1967 Don Cardwell (*New York Mets*). A 3.57 ERA, 1.276 WHIP, and three shutouts helped.

1967 Bob Hendley (*New York Mets*). Hendley's stats weren't bad at all (3.44 ERA, 1.316 WHIP).

Sort of Random Trivia: Hall of Fame pitcher Nolan Ryan broke into the majors with the Mets in 1966. Early in his career, his fingers would develop blisters after hurling five innings or so. To combat this, Ryan would soak his digits in pickle brine. As time went on, his fingers toughened up, and he stopped the practice. From then on, opposing batters were in a "pickle," having to face Ryan's blazing fastball for a full nine.

1968 No 100 loss teams.

1969 Rusty Staub (*Montreal Expos 52-110*). One of the best outfielders in the NL as a member of the Astros for several years, acquired by the Expos before the season. The man Canadian fans dubbed "Le Grande Orange" delivered in a big way. He batted .302 with a .426 on-base percentage, plus he blasted 29 home runs and slugged at a .526 clip.

1969 Mack Jones (*Montreal Expos*). After delivering a home run and triple in Montreal's debut game, a portion of the leftfield stands at Jarry Park was dubbed "Jonesville" by the fans. Jones finished the season with a .279 AVG, 22 HR, and 79 RBI.

1969 Coco Laboy (*Montreal Expos*). I love that name! His OBP (.308) was terrible, BUT he did drill 18 home runs, ripped 29 doubles, and led the club with 83 RBI.

1969 Bob Bailey (*Montreal Expos*). Bailey appeared in 111 games and put up respectable stats (.265 AVG, .337 OBP, 53 RBI). Honorable Mention.

1969 A few guys (*Montreal Expos*). INBB Award for pitcher Gary Waslewski (3.29 ERA) and an Honorable Mentions for Roy Face (3.94 ERA, 1.298 WHIP). The staff finished with a bad 4.33 ERA; none of Mauch's hurlers recorded anything resembling an outstanding season, but Gary and Roy didn't humiliate themselves, either.

Do I get too chummy when I use the players' first names? I don't think so, but I'd really like to know what you think. Send your letters and post cards to my administrative assistant, S. Claus, at:

1225 Workshop Lane
North Pole, Alaska
99705

1969 Nate Colbert (*San Diego Padres 52-100*). The center of the Padres offensive attack during the first few years of the franchise, Colbert smashed 24 home runs as a rookie in 1969. Over the next four seasons, the muscular righty swinger powered 38, 27, 38, and 22 long balls. His 66 RBI during that first season is impressive, considering that not many of his teammates were getting on base ahead of him.

1969 Al Ferrara (*San Diego Padres*). After being a bencher for several seasons with the Dodgers, Ferrara was finally given a chance to be an everyday player with the Padres and made the most of it. In 1969, Ferrara hit .260, got on base at a .349 clip, belted 14 home runs, and plated 61 runners.

1969 Ollie Brown (*San Diego Padres*). An underachiever with the Giants, Brown blossomed in 1969 with 20 HR and 61 RBI. The man had a rifle arm and registered 14 outfield assists, the 3rd highest total in the NL. Also, owner of one of the era's most famous nicknames, "Downtown."

1969 Dick Kelley (*San Diego Padres*). Besides an anemic offensive attack, the expansion Padres were also woeful in the pitching department. One exception was veteran lefty Dick Kelley who allowed just 113 hits and struck out 96 in 136 innings pitched. During a seven-year career that ended in 1971, Kelley's lifetime ERA and WHIP were good (3.39, 1.285), but his record was an abysmal 18-30. His former team, the Braves, were mediocre in 1967 and 1968, and it's probable that he lost a few games with Atlanta that he might have won with a better club.

1969 Joe Niekro (San Diego Padres). He lost 17 games, but his ERA wasn't too bad (3.70) with a WHIP of 1.227. In 203 innings pitched, he allowed just 45 walks and 15 home runs. Niekro wouldn't retire until

1988 at the age of 43; he was one of the most consistent pitchers of the pre-steroid era, averaging 13 wins a season.

Well, folks, that ends the INBB rundown for a glorious decade of the first man on the moon, the Beatles, flower power, and draft card burning.

Peace and love!

A's first sacker Norn Siebern drove-in 98 runs in 1961. (tradingcarddb.com)

In 1961, Philly's young outfielder Johnny Callison established himself as an offensive threat. (tradingcarddb.com)

Slugger Billy Williams is INBB worthy with the bat and glove. (tradingcarddb.com)

Hurler Claude Osteen was one of the only pitchers the Senators could count on in 1962. (tradingcarddb.com)

Veteran Don Caldwell helped stabilize a young Mets pitching staff. (Courtesy East Hills Shopping Center)

Phil Niekro's brother Joe was a talented pitcher, too. (tradingcarddb.com)

America and the world was shocked when President Kennedy was assassinated in November 1963. (Courtesy Warren Commission Exhibit #697)

Dr. Martin Luther King was a civil rights champion in the 1960s. (Courtesy National Archives)

The 1970s

Have a Nice Day!

Some important stuff that happened in the 1970s:

- The United States began establishing formal diplomatic relations with Communist China when President Nixon visited the Asian country in February 1972.

- The U.S. Senate passed the Equal Rights Amendment in March 1972. The legislation was designed to ban sex-based discrimination. The amendment ultimately failed to gain the approval of the ¾ of the states and is never added to the U.S. Constitution.

- In October 1973, OPEC stopped importing oil to the U.S. in an effort to end military and financial support for the State of Israel. Americans felt the pinch with long lines at the pumps, gas shortages, and escalating prices.

- U.S. President Richard Nixon resigned from office on August 8, 1974. Congressional hearings had revealed that Nixon had lied about and tried to cover up a politically motivated burglary at the Watergate Hotel in 1972.

- On April 30, 1975, the Vietnam War ended when the U.S. completes the withdrawal of military personnel from South Vietnam.

- Two unsuccessful assassination attempts, 17 days apart, were made on the life of U.S. President Gerald Ford in September 1975.

- The United States celebrated the 200th anniversary of the signing of the Declaration of Independence on July 4, 1976.

• Iranian revolutionaries successfully attacked the U.S. Embassy in Tehran on November 4, 1979, and took 90 hostages. The crisis lasted until January 1981, when the hostages are released the day Ronald Reagan was sworn in to be president.

Some important stuff that happened in Major League Baseball in the 1970s:

• Before the 1970 season, the Seattle Pilots relocated to Milwaukee and became the Brewers.

• The American League adopted the Designated Hitter rule for 1973, allowing teams to use a hitter in place of the pitcher in the batting order. Offensive statistics in the Junior Circuit exploded as a result.

• The man who broke baseball's color line in 1947, Jackie Robinson, died in October 1972.

• Loaded with mustaches, wild characters, and talent, Charles Finley's Oakland A's captured three straight World Championships (1972-1974).

• Slugger Hank Aaron took Dodgers' pitcher Al Downing deep in April 1974 and broke Babe Ruth's career record of 714 home runs

• The era of free agency commenced in 1975 when arbitrator Peter Seitz ruled that owners do not own and control players' contracts in perpetuity.

• Nicknamed "The Big Red Machine," the Cincinnati Reds won back-to-back World Series (1975 and 1976).

• After being down Three games to one, the Pittsburgh Pirates, led by 39-year-old Willie "Pops" Stargell, won the 1979 World Series over the Baltimore Orioles.

◆ ◆ ◆

De stats, Boss! De stats! The 1970s were not without with its' share of INBB-worthy players. Some of the names may have been forgotten but not by the Committee.

1970 Gail Hopkins *(Chicago White Sox 56-106)*. Over 116 games, the first sacker batted .286 and fielded a nifty .987. His power numbers were low (only 25 extra-base hits), but he did manage to get on base at a decent clip (.346 OBP).

1970 Luis Aparicio *(Chicago White Sox)*. Despite their woeful record, the Pale Hose had some guys who could hit. Slick fielding shortstop Luis Aparicio registered a cool .313 AVG and .372 OBP.

1970 Bill Melton *(Chicago White Sox)*. The 6'2", 200-pound masher blasted 33 circuit clouts and knocked in 96.

1970 Carlos May *(Chicago White Sox)*. National League slugger Lee May's brother got on base at a .373 rate, scored 83 runs, and drove in 68. He only committed two errors in 141 games as an outfielder and nailed 12 runners trying to take an extra-base—a two-time All-Star.

1970 Ken Berry *(Chicago White Sox)*. The Kansas City native hit .276 and registered the 2nd highest OBP of his 14-year-career (.344). He also knocked in 50 runs.

1970 Tommy John *(Chicago White Sox)*. Not many bright spots on a pitching staff that finished with a 4.54 ERA. Lefty Tommy John was one with 12 wins, a 3.27 ERA, and 1.314 WHIP over 269 innings of work. Two thumbs-up and a virtual pat on the back for John.

1970 Wilbur Wood *(Chicago White Sox)*. A year before Chicago decided to use "Wilbah" as a starter, Wood was the team's closer. His 21 saves were sixth-best in the AL, and a 2.81 ERA distinguished him far above any of his south side mound mates. That fluttering knuckleball of his also helped Wood earn nine wins, the third-highest total on the team.

Sort of Random Trivia: On June 12, 1970, Pittsburgh Pirate pitcher Doc Ellis threw a no-hitter against the San Diego Padres. A colorful character, Ellis claims he was tripping on LSD at the time. He says, "I was as high as a Georgia pine."

"All I could tell is if they (the batters) were on the right side or the left side," Ellis revealed. "The catcher had tape on his fingers to help me see signals."

1971 Nate Colbert *(San Diego Padres 61-100)*. The expansion Padres first major star, Colbert, nabbed s his 2nd INBB with 27 HR, 84 RBI, and 81 runs scored. A tough, gritty player, the first baseman slammed five home runs in a doubleheader against the Braves in 1972 after injuring his knee the night before.

1971 Ollie Brown *(San Diego Padres)*, "Downtown" Ollie did alright with a .273 AVG, .346 OBP, 9 HR, and 55 RBI. Brown was San Diego's first pick in the 1969 expansion draft after spending the first four years of his career with the Giants.

1971 Dave Roberts *(San Diego Padres)*. Manager Preston Gomez's ace pitcher, Roberts, blossomed into one of the best hurlers in the NL. While pitching for the worst team in the league, the big lefty won 14, posted a 2.10 ERA and 1.109 WHIP. He also completed 14 games.

1971 Clay Kirby *(San Diego Padres)*. Another bright spot in a dismal season for the denizens of Jack Murphy Stadium. Kirby probably should be considered co-ace with Roberts. His line: 15-13, 2.83 ERA, 1.182 WHIP, and 13 complete games.

1971 Steve Arlin *(San Diego Padres)*. Arlin brought home an INBB for nine wins, 3.48 ERA, and 10 complete games.

1971 Fred Norman *(San Diego Padres)*. It's an INBB for Norman, too. His ERA (3.32) was good, and WHIP (1.335) quite satisfactory. He deserved better than that 3-12 record.

1971 Dick Kelley *(San Diego Padres)*. Kelley's last season in the big leagues. His career might have lasted longer, but chronic tendinitis in 1972 hampered his effectiveness and led to his release. The Rangers picked him up and sent him to their AAA team, where he pitched poorly in nine games and then retired.

For his work in 1971 (3.47 ERA, 1.257 WHIP, 42 K in 60 IP), the future founder of "The Dick Kelley Pitching School" takes the brass ring.

1972 Ted Ford *(Texas Rangers 54-100)*. Honorable Mention. The Rangers' offense in 1972 was stinkaroo. They finished last out of 12 teams in BA,

OBP, H, and HR. Outfielder Ted Ford ripped 14 long balls and knocked in 50 runs. A mediocre .235 average kept him from winning the "Big Enchilada." (Don't you just love it when people who write sports books use descriptive phrases like "Big Enchilada"?)

1972 A Bunch of Guys *(Texas Rangers)*. Five Ranger hurlers were worthy of exceedingly prestigious INBB Awards, and one secured an Honorable Mention.

Winners of the INBB:

1. Dick Brown (8-10, 3.63 ERA, 1.333 WHIP)
2. Mike Paul (8-9, 2.17 ERA, 1.243 WHIP)
3. Horacio Pina (3.20 ERA, 15 saves, 1.368 WHIP)
4. Paul Linblad (2.62 ERA, 9 saves, 1.244 WHIP)
5. Jim Shellenback (3.47 ERA and 1.088 WHIP over 60 innings)

And the Honorable Mention goes to . . .

Rich Hand (10-14, 3.32 ERA, 1.418 WHIP). Hand led the staff in victories, but that walks-per-innings-pitched ratio is high, thanks to 103 walks issued over 171 innings.

1973 Nate Colbert *(San Diego Padres 60-102)*. The third INBB for Nathan; if this keeps up, we might need to change the name of the award to "The Nate Colbert Award for Excellence in the Midst of Absolute Baseball Yuckiness." It would be affectionately known as the NCAEMABY.

Hmmm. That's a lot of letters to deal with.

It doesn't exactly roll off the tongue, does it?

Colbert's line in 1972: (.270 AVG, .343 OBP, 22 HR, 80 RBI)

1973 Another Bunch of Guys *(San Diego Padres)*.

Manager Don Zimmer had some gentleman at his disposal who generated a few runs. These position players win INBBs:

1. Dave Roberts (.286 AVG, 21 HR, 64 RBI)
2. Johnny Grubb (.311 AVG, .373 OBP)
3. Jerry Morales (.281 AVG, 23 doubles, 9 HR in 388 at-bats)
4. Fred Kendall (.282 AVG, 10 HR, 59 RBI)
5. Cito Gaston (16 HR, 57 RBI)

San Diego's pitching staff was bad, but two lads excelled (I found the word "lads" in my Thesaurus. I gotta keep word usage fresh and lively.)

Earning INBBs are:

Bill Grief (10-17, 3.21 ERA, 1.219 WHIP)
Randy Jones (7-6, 3.16, 1.189 WHIP)

Jones would soon become the staff ace. He made his MLB debut in June 1973.

1973 Dave Nelson *(Texas Rangers 57-105)*. Two thumbs-up and a hearty pat on the back for Nelson and his .286 AVG, 43 steals, and 71 runs scored.

1973 Jeff Burroughs *(Texas Rangers)*. A first-round draft pick in 1969, Burroughs cracked the starting line-up in 1973 and delivered 30 HR and 85 RBI. His .279 AVG and .355 OBP were none too shabby, either.

1973 Alex Johnson *(Texas Rangers)*. The Committee was tempted only to honor Johnson with an Honorable Mention. At first glance, his .287 AVG seems kind-of-empty with only 37 extra-base hits over 158 games. However, he did drive in 68 and score 62 runs, figures that carry him just over the line into the magical land of INBB.

1973 Jim Bibby *(Texas Rangers)*. Traded by the Cardinals to the Rangers in June, the rookie right-hander was plugged into the starting rotation and did not disappoint. Over a little more than half a season, Bibby won nine games, recorded a 3.24 ERA, completed 11 games, and fanned 155 batters over 180 innings.

1973 Sonny Siebert *(Texas Rangers)*. The two-time All-Star was near the end of his career in 1973. It wasn't a bad season for a 105-loss club (7-11, 3.99 ERA, 1.312 WHIP) but not stellar. Honorable Mention.

1974 Willie McCovey *(San Diego Padres 60-102)*. Baseball fans in Bay Area had a hard time coping with the sight of "Stretch" in anything but a Giants uniform. San Francisco had traded him to the Padres after the 1973 campaign, thinking the big guy's tank was empty. The 36-year-old

McCovey proved them wrong, delivering 22 HR, 63 RBI, .506 SLG, and .416 OBP in 443 plate appearances. The man kept producing and realizing the error of their ways. The Giants reacquired him in 1977. By the time he retired three years later, Willie had amassed 521 home runs and eventually would be a first-year eligible Hall of Fame selection in 1986.

1974 Dave Winfield *(San Diego Padres)*. A 40th round draft pick by the Orioles, the future superstar, played well in his first full season in the big show; he pounded 20 HR and delivered 75 RBI. The best was yet to come.

1974 Nate Colbert *(San Diego Padres)*. A pitiful .207 BA was somewhat redeemed by 14 HR and 54 RBI over 119 games. The few hits he got were productive. Honorable Mention.

The 1974 Padres pitching staff was awful. No INBBs, no Honorable Mentions, no nothing!

1974 Willie Horton *(Detroit Tigers 57-102)*. The 32-year-old Designated Hitter did fine with a .275 AVG, 25 HR, and 92 RBI. Nobody else on the Tigers came close to his numbers.

1975 Aurelio Rodriguez *(Detroit Tigers)*. Honorable Mention for 13 fence-clearing long balls and 60 RBI. As a third baseman, he committed 25 errors, but he got to a lot of balls that other guys didn't; he led the AL in range factor (3.53) and is 4th on the all-time list in the same category (3.189).

1975 Bill Freehan *(Detroit Tigers)*. A hold-over from the legendary 1968 team that won the World Championship. At the age of 33, Freehan caught 113 games and was named to his 11th All-Star Team. The durable receiver nabbed an Honorable Mention for his 14 HR and 47 RBI.

1975 Mickey Lolich *(Detroit Tigers)*. Along with winning 12 games, the portly left-hander completed 19 games and posted a 3.78 ERA. Not outstanding stats, but compared to most of the rest of the staff, they look like prime Koufax numbers. (I guess that last statement sounds like exaggerated hyperbole. Look, I need to lay controversial stuff on you from time to time to stir things up, OK?)

1975 John Hiller *(Detroit Tigers)*. The Canadian import posted outstanding figures (2.17 ERA, 14 SV, 1.245 WHIP, 87 K in 71 innings). Can there be any doubt that the man deserved an INBB?

1976 Steve Rogers *(Montreal Expos 55-107)*. No Expo positional player performed well enough to garner either an INBB or Honorable Mention, but three of the team's pitchers did. The club's ace, Steve Rogers, is one (3.21 ERA, 1.222 WHIP, four shutouts). A poor 7-17 record was almost entirely attributable to the clowns surrounding him when he pitched.
   Woodie Fryman (13 wins, 3.37 ERA, and 1.359 WHIP).
   Dale Murray (3.26 ERA, 1.359 WHIP, 14 saves).

1977 Otto Velez *(Toronto Blue Jays 54-107)*. Despite the abysmal record, the Blue Jays fielded a few decent players during their inaugural season. Outfielder Otto Velez stroked 16 home runs, drove in 66 runs, and sported a .366 OBP. The American League "Player of the Month" for April 1977.

1977 Ron Fairly *(Toronto Blue Jays)*. In his last season as a regular, the 38-year-old Fairly batted .279 with a .362 OBP, hit 19 HR, and recorded 64 RBI. He would retire after the 1978 season, ending a 21-year-career.

1977 Bob Bailor *(Toronto Blue Jays)*. Bailor served as a Jays' utility man, putting in time at all three outfield positions, shortstop and DH. His .310 AVG was 2nd highest on the team, and Bailor's 15 steals were tops on the club.

1977 Al Woods *(Toronto Blue Jays)*. As a rookie in 1977, Woods hit .284, the highest average of his career. A respectable .336 OBP helped the man walk away with one of those darn INBB Awards.

1977 Mike Willis *(Toronto Blue Jays)*. Taken from the Orioles roster in the expansion draft, Willis pitched 107 innings with fair results (3.94 ERA, 1.332 WHIP, five saves). Fifteen home runs surrendered blemish his record a bit. Honorable Mention.

1977 Pete Vukovich *(Toronto Blue Jays)*. Sort of the Blue Jays closer, although he did start eight games, Pete struck out 123 (over 148 innings), put up a 3.47 ERA, 1.365 WHIP, and eight saves.

1977 Biff Pocoroba *(Atlanta Braves 61-101)*. The man with one of the all-time great names in baseball history, Biff Pocoroba did a first-rate job behind the plate and hit .290 with a .394 OBP. "Biff" is his real first name and not a nickname.

1977 Willie Montanez *(Atlanta Braves)*. His first name was actually "Guillermo." (Lots of interesting stuff here, don't you think?) A productive player for most of his career, Willie batted .287 in 1977 and blasted 20 home runs and 31 doubles. Always a highly proficient glove man, his fielding percentage was a sparkling .992. He was named to the National League All-Star team for the first and only time in his career.

1977 Gary Matthews *(Atlanta Braves)*. An underrated outfielder, Matthews had a rifle arm and was among the top ten in assists nine in times during his career. A good hitter, Matthews contributed a .283 BA and 17 HR to Atlanta's cause. He could steal a base for you, too. He swiped 22 and was only thrown out six times in 1977.

1977 Jeff Burroughs *(Atlanta Braves)*. In 1970, Ted Williams called Burroughs "The greatest young hitter I've ever seen." High praise from a guy who knew a thing or two about making contact and getting on base. Back problems would eventually diminish Burroughs' production, but in 1977 the Long Beach, California native was firing on all cylinders (41 HR, 114 RBI).

1977 Dave Campbell *(Atlanta Braves)*. The rookie was INBB worthy on a crappy team, saving 13 games while recording a 3.05 ERA and 1.252 WHIP. The future looked bright, but control problems would plague Campbell in 1978 (49 walks/69 innings), and he was traded to the Expos in the off-season. He never returned to the majors, spending the next three years with Montreal's top farm team, the Denver Bears.

1978 Bob Stinson *(Seattle Mariners 56-104)*. Seattle's starting catcher batted .258, hit 11 home runs, and drove in 55 runs. Not outstanding numbers, but they look good on a club that finished near the bottom in runs scored, hits, home runs, batting average, and on-base percentage. Honorable Mention.

1978 Craig Reynolds *(Seattle Mariners)*. Reynolds hit .292 and made the AL All-Star team. The Committee almost gave him an Honorable Mention instead of an INBB because he committed 29 errors and fielded a less than wonderful .960. But the comment about Aurelio Rodriguez also applies here; Reynolds was 4th in the league in range factor and handled a lot of balls that others would not have gotten to.

1978 Bruce Bochte *(Seattle Mariners)*. The comment about teammate Stinson applies here as well. His line of .263 AVG, .342 OBP, 11 HR, and 51 RBI on a weak-hitting team like the Mariners ain't bad. Honorable Mention.

(I hope I haven't been using the phrase "applies here" too many times. It just seems to fit, and to be honest, I can't think of something better to say.)

1978 Leon Roberts *(Seattle Mariners)*. This fella had an outstanding year in 1978. Along with batting .301, he smacked 22 home runs and recorded 92 RBI, stats that contributed heavily to a lofty .515 slugging percentage. By far his best season in major leagues (.267 lifetime AVG), Roberts received a little support for American League MVP.

1978 Enrique Romo *(Seattle Mariners)*. The Mariner's closer, Romo managed to succeed on a staff that floundered with a collective 4.67 ERA. His 3.69 ERA was OK, but that 1.183 WHIP was great. The Committee was also impressed by Romo's ten saves on a club that didn't present him with many opportunities to protect late-inning leads.

1978 John Mayberry *(Toronto Blue Jays 59-102)*. Big John took his first INBB with 22 HR and 70 RBI.

1978 Roy Howell (Toronto Blue Jays). Did you know that for a few seasons in the 1940s, the Philadelphia Phillies attempted to change the club's nickname to "Blue Jays"? It's true. What does this have to do with the Jays' third sacker? Nothing really. I just thought you'd appreciate a little trivia thrown in here. Howell was second on the team in RBI (61), and his .270 AVG was twenty points higher than Toronto's average as a whole diamond ensemble.

(Hey, how do you like that phrase "diamond ensemble"? Pretty sweet, huh? Not bad for a hack writer, isn't it?)

1978 Tom Murphy *(Toronto Blue Jays).* In his next-to-last season in the Majors, the veteran hurler posted a 3.69 ERA. Everyone else on the staff that pitched 50 or more innings put up ERAs ranging from 4.24-6.26. His 1.331 WHIP was decent.

NOTE: Toronto's Victor Cruz had a fine year (1.71 ERA, ten saves) but only pitched 47 innings. The cut-off for INBB consideration is 50 innings, a benchmark implemented after much contemplation by the Committee. We apologize, but we must have standards and do not feel guilty about denying Cruz an award.
Well, at least not *too* guilty . . .

1979 Dave Revering *(1979 Oakland A's 54-108).* There wasn't much to cheer for at Oakland-Alameda Coliseum during the lost summer of 1979. Only 306,763 hardy folks dared to pass through the turnstiles to witness the diamond disaster. First baseman Dave Revering showed the minuscule crowds what a real big-league player looks like. He batted .288, blasted 19 home runs, and recorded 77 RBI.

1979 Jeff Newman *(Oakland A's).* Catcher Newman did himself proud with 22 HR and 71 RBI. For his work, he earned a spot on the 1979 American League All-Star team.

1979 Wayne Gross *(Oakland A's).* Honorable Mention. He did hit 14 homers and plated 50 teammates but was a lousy third baseman with a .943 fielding percentage.
Not a single A's hurler merited an INBB or Honorable Mention. Oakland's offensive attack was so-so, but the pitching staff was brutal with a 4.75 ERA and a league-leading 654 walks issued.

1979 John Mayberry *(Toronto Blue Jays 53-109).* It was another good season for Mayberry and another INBB (.274 AVG, .372 OBP, 21 HR, 74 RBI). In addition, he fielded his position (1B) well, committing only six errors in 1272 chances.

1979 Alfredo Griffin *(Toronto Blue Jays)*. The 1979 co-winner of the AL Rookie of the Year, the speedy shortstop, led the team in steals with 21, scored 81 runs, and batted a swell .287.

1979 Al Woods *(Toronto Blue Jays)*. A native of Oakland, California, Woods didn't allow the swirling commode that was the Blue Jays' season suck him down. A .278 AVG, .337 OBP, and 24 doubles kept things cool (and dry).

1979 Roy Howell *(Toronto Blue Jays)*. It's INBB #2 for Howell (15 HR, 72 RBI).

1979 Rico Carty *(Toronto Blue Jays)*. Once one of the most feared hitters in baseball, the"Beeg Mon" played in 152 games and closed out a fine 15-year career with a .256 AVG, 12 HR, and 55 RBI. It was way below his prime output but good enough to win an Honorable Mention.

1979 Tom Underwood *(Toronto Blue Jays)*. The lefty was the ace of Roy Hartfield's beleaguered pitching staff with this line: 3.69 ERA, 1.357 WHIP, 12 complete games.

1979 Dave Lemanczyk *(Toronto Blue Jays)*. I hope I spelled the man's last name correctly. Like Underwood, "What's His Name" was an overachiever with a 3.71 ERA, 1.273 WHIP, and 11 complete games.

That Blue Jays staff ERA of 4.75 in 1979 made Underwood's and Lemanczyk's ERA look good.

1979 Tom Buskey *(Toronto Blue Jays)*. The 32-year-old closer finished 40 games but only recorded seven saves. Lack of save opportunities kept his number down; he entered numerous games when the Blue Jays were behind and eventually lost. His 3.43 ERA was the lowest on the team, as was his 1.258 WHIP. Buskey was not a "Baseball Bozo" in 1979.

Speedy Dave Nelson swiped 43 bases for the Rangers in 1973. (tradingcarddb.com)

INBB for Jeff Burroughs for his work in 1973 (30 HR, 85 RBI). (tradingcarddb.com)

Future superstar Dave Winfield was a 40th round draft choice in 1969. Now, that's scouting! (tradkingcarddb.com)

The star of the 1968 World Series, Mickey Lolich, was still going strong in 1975. (tradingcarddb.com)

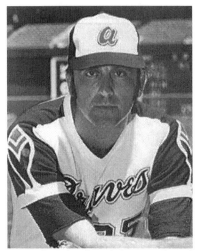

Joe Niekro's brother Phil was a talented pitcher, too. (tradingcarddb.com)

Willie Montanez was a flashy and sometimes cocky player but he backed up the act with solid numbers and a sure glove. (tradingcarddb.com)

One-time ardent anti-Communist Richard Nixon worked to open-up relations with mainland China in the early 1970s. (Courtesy Rirchard Nixon Presidential Library and Museum)

In 1976, America celebrated the 200th anniversary of it's founding with gusto! (Courtesy U.S. Department of Agriculture)

The 1980s

Go out there and lose one for the Gipper!

Some important stuff that happened in the 1980s:

- A major volcanic eruption took place at Mount St. Helen's in Washington State on May 21, 1980. Tons of volcanic ash were blasted 80,000 feet into the air and eventually blanketed 11 states. It's estimated that the event caused one billion dollars in damages and resulted in the deaths of 57.

- In November 1980, Conservative Republican Ronald Reagan defeated Democrat Jimmy Carter to become the 40th President of the United States.

- Former Beatle John Lennon was shot to death by a mentally unstable loner in front of the musician's New York apartment building on December 8, 1980.

- As President Regan is sworn in to begin a first term, Iran releases the 52 American hostages it held for 444 days. The date was January 20, 1981.

- On February 28, 1983, 125 million people tuned in to watch the final episode of the long-running TV series *M.A.S.H.*

- Motorola introduced the first mobile phone to the U.S. Market in 1983.

- The U.S. Space Shuttle Challenger exploded 73 seconds after liftoff from Cape Canaveral, Florida, killing all seven on board. The tragedy occurred on January 28, 1986.

- The antidepressant Prozac became available as a prescription in 1987.

- In May 1989, China declared martial law and sent troops and tanks to forcefully disperse thousands of students protesting for freedom at

Tiananmen Square in Beijing. The crackdown resulted in 241 deaths and approximately 7,000 wounded.

- A symbol of the Cold War, the Berlin Wall, was torn down on November 9, 1989. Almost a year later, East and West Germany merged to become the Federal Republic of Germany.

Some important stuff that happened in Major League Baseball in the 1980s:

- In the 1980 World Series, the Philadelphia Phillies captured their first World Championship when they downed the Kansas City Royals in six games.

- Major League baseball players went on strike on June 12, 1981. A settlement is reached in late July after 713 games have been canceled. The season resumed on August 9th.

- Legendary pitcher Leroy Satchell Paige passed away on June 8, 1982. Paige himself estimated that he had pitched in about 2,500 games over a career that started in 1926.

- The International Olympic Committee (I.O.C.) restored the gold medals that Jim Thorpe won seven decades earlier. They had been stripped from the star athlete because he had played a couple of seasons of semi-pro baseball at a salary of 60 dollars a month.

- In 1986, seven players were suspended conditionally for one year by Commissioner Peter Ueberroth for lying while under oath at hearings the previous year about cocaine trafficking. The players are Dale Berra, Lonnie Smith, Jeff Leonard, Enos Cabell, Dave Parker, Joaquin Andujar, and Keith Hernandez.

- Also, in 1986, the I.O.C. voted to approve baseball as a medal sport beginning in 1992.

- On a late-night news program in April 1987, Dodger General Manager Al Campanis stunned the moderator and viewers when he said African Americans don't have the "mental faculties" to be in management positions. A firestorm of criticism and outrage follow; Campanis is fired two days later.

- In 1988, The CBS network paid 1.1 billion dollars for the exclusive rights to telecast baseball from 1990-1994.

- ◆ A. Bartlett Giamatti assumed the duties of Major League Baseball's Commissioner on April 1, 1989. His tenure would be short; five months later, he died from a massive heart attack at Martha's Vineyard at the age of 51.

- ◆ Eight days before Giamatti's death, baseball's all-time hit leader, Pete Rose, is banished for life for gambling on games his team played in

◆ ◆ ◆

There are many INBB Award winners and more than a few Honorable Mentions to toast for the 1980s. The teams they played for were horrible to the umpteenth power!

1980 Bruce Bochte *(Seattle Mariners 59–103 record)*. First baseman Bochte managed to hit .300 with an impressive .381 OBP. He also clubbed 34 doubles and 13 home runs while driving in 78.
Bruce, this "INBB" is for you!

1981 There was a lengthy strike, so there were no 100-loss teams.

1982 Kent Hrbek *(Minnesota Twins 60–102 record)*. Another first base-man, the 22-year-old Hrbek hit 23 home runs, batted .301, and knocked in 92 runs to the delight of the beleaguered Twins' faithful. The 1982 club was young and, within five years, would mature to win the American League pennant and the World Series.

1982 Tom Brunansky *(Minnesota Twins)*. Brunansky (age 21) gave the Twins and their followers plenty of realistic hope for the future. The out-fielder slugged 20 home runs, hit 30 doubles, and compiled a lofty .377 OBP. His .848 OPS tied Hrbek for the highest percentage on the team.

1982 Gary Ward *(Minnesota Twins)*. Veteran outfielder Gary Ward regis-tered a .289 average to go along with 28 dingers and 91 ribbies (Don't you just love it when we use baseball slang? Timeless stuff like "dingers" and "ribbies"?).

1982 Gary Gaetti (Minnesota Twins) The 23-year-old Gaetti of the Twins earned an INBB with his 25 home run and 84 RBI performance in 1982. The batting average was low (.230), but the power numbers were sweet.

1982 Bobby Castillo *(Minnesota Twins)* Castillo was the only pitcher on the Minnesota staff worth anything in 1982. His line was good: 13–11, 3.66 ERA, 123 K in 218.2 innings, 1.276 WHIP. The entire staff finished 14th (out of 14 teams) in earned runs, ERA, and walks allowed. They managed to climb up to 13th place in the league in home runs surrendered.

1982 Dan Driessen *(Cincinnati Reds 60–101 record)*. Yet another first sacker won an INBB (This must mean something, but what?). His .269 average was OK, but he did draw 82 walks that contributed to a good .368 on-base percentage. No singles hitter, Driessen ripped 17 home runs and 25 doubles amid the carnage that was a 100 plus loss season for the Red Legs.

1982 Cesar Cedeno *(Cincinnati Reds)*. He stroked a .289 average and 57 RBI on a team that didn't put a whole lot of runners on base ahead of him. His OBP was a respectable .346. A top-notch defensive outfielder, Cedeno committed only three errors in 132 games.

1982 Dave Concepcion *(Cincinnati Reds)*. One of the last vestiges of Cincy's "Big Red Machine" of the 1970s, the 34-year-old infielder produced the second-highest batting average for a regular on the team (.287) and finished third in the league in overall fielding percentage (.977) for shortstops.

1982 Mario Soto *(Cincinnati Reds)*. His so-so 14–13 record was due mainly to lack of support from teammates and not his pitching. No siree. In 257innings, Soto fanned 274 and allowed only 202 hits. His excellent ERA and WHIP numbers (2.79 and 1.060) helped place Mario among baseball's elite hurlers in 1982. The rest of Cincy's rotation went a combined 22–44 as the team claimed their place in the NL Western Division cellar.

1983 Steve Henderson *(Seattle Mariners, 60–102)*. You can't blame the team's record on the man from Houston, Texas (I guess you *could* blame him, this is a free country, go for it. But if you ask me, that would be totally unfair). Henderson delivered a .294 AVG and .356 OBP for a woeful Mariners club. The outfielder also slashed 32 doubles and recorded 55 RBI.

1983 Matt Young *(Seattle Mariners)*. The ace of a mediocre pitching staff, Young was one of the league's better pitchers in 1983. His 11–15 record belied a total stat package that included a 3.27 era, just 178 hits in 203 innings pitched, 130 K, and a 1.262 WHIP.

1983 *Another* First Baseman *(Seattle Mariners)*. The "Big One" goes to Pat Putnam of the Mariners, who drilled 19 home runs and drove in 67 runs in 1983. He handled his position well, too, finishing with a terrific fielding percentage (.994).

1984 No 100-loss teams.

1985 Joe Orsulak *(Pittsburgh Pirates 57–104)*. Over 121 games played, the singles-hitting outfielder logged a .300 AVG, .342 OBP, and stole 24 bases (The Pirates collectively hit .255).

1985 Johnny Ray *(Pittsburgh Pirates)*. Veteran second baseman pleased Pirate faithful with 70 RBI. Ray also drilled 33 doubles and struck out only 24 times in 652 plate appearances.

1985 Rick Reuschel *(Pittsburgh Pirates)*. While just about everything in the Steel City was crashing in around him, the chubby one put in an excellent season. His record was 14–8 with a fantastic 2.27 ERA and a tiny 1.057 WHIP. In 194 innings, he surrendered just 153 hits and struck out 130.

1985 Cecilio Guante *(Pittsburgh Pirates)*. A richly deserved INBB Award for Sir Cecilio. In 1985, he posted a 2.72 ERA, allowed just 84 hits in 109 innings, fanned 92, and finished with a 1.138 WHIP. As a staff, the Pirates finished at or near the bottom in almost every category. Of course, that kind of thing usually happens when a team loses 104 games, doesn't it?

1985 Tony Bernazard *(Cleveland Indians 60–102)*. The Tribe second baseman earned an INBB based on his .274 AVG, .361 OBP, 59 RBI, and 17 steals. His 11 home runs were quite conspicuous on a club that didn't hit many long balls; Cleveland finished 13th out of 14 teams in home runs (116).

1985 Julio Franco *(Cleveland Indians)*. This guy persevered through his club's mounting losses by hitting .288 and driving in 99 runs. Franco was kinda like a baseball version of the long-running TV show, NCIS. How long has that been on the air? Since the Lyndon Johnson Administration?

Don't get me wrong, I love the show and watch it every week. I mean, I know most of Gibbs' rules *by heart*. But it has been on for an extended period. Anyhow, Franco was in his fourth season as a major leaguer at the time; he would toil for another 19 years before retiring.

1985 Brett Butler *(Cleveland Indians)*. A genuinely outstanding player who was highly productive during a 17-year career in the big leagues. The 665,181 long-suffering fans that went through the turnstiles at Municipal Stadium in 1985 had the privilege of watching one of the game's best. Throughout that disastrous campaign, the swift Butler hit .311, swatted 14 triples, and stole 44 bases. His .377 OBP was impressive, and 50 RBI were outstanding for a lead-off hitter. If anyone deserved an INBB Award for the 1980s, it was Brett Butler in 1985.

1985 Bert Blyleven *(Cleveland Indians)*. Over 179 innings of work, Blyleven fanned 129 batters, a total that was quite noticeable on a staff that finished last overall in strikeouts. His record was only 9–11, but he deserved better with a 3.26 ERA and 15 complete games. Reality bites sometimes, doesn't it? Nobody else on the team had an ERA below 3.92, and his fellow starting pitchers sported earned run averages of 4.90, 5.34, 6.01, and 6.68.

1985 Chris Brown *(San Francisco Giants 62–100)*. With a not-so-bad .271 batting average, an equally not-so-bad .345 OBP, almost impressive 16 home runs, and kind of decent 61 RBIs, the Giants' third baseman earned one of those really wonderful INBBs.

1985 Chili Davis *(San Francisco Giants)*. His line: .270 AVG, .349 OBP, 13 HRs, and 56 RBI. Just like teammate Brown, his sort of good stats lifted him to one of those coveted INBB Awards.

1985 Mike Krukow *(San Francisco Giants)*. Never mind the 8–11 record (see the Bert Blyleven comments). Check out the 150 K in 194 innings pitched, 1.156 WHIP, and decent 3.38 ERA. The Giants right-hander was another solid pitcher stuck on a lousy team.

1985 Scott Garrelts *(San Francisco Giants)*. One of baseball's best relievers in 1985, Garrelts allowed just 76 hits in 105 innings pitched and surrendered just two home runs.

1985 Mark Davis (San Francisco Giants) In 114 innings, Davis struck out 113 and allowed only 89 hits.

1985 Jeff Leonard *(San Francisco Giants).* The outfielder cracked 17 home runs, drove in 62, and swiped 11 bases in 1985. A middling .241 batting average and terrible .272 OBP kept the guy nicknamed "Old Penitentiary Face" from winning an INBB outright. Honorable Mention.

I wonder why they called him "Old Penitentiary Face." I've seen photos of the man. Doesn't

look like a crook to me. Just sayin' . . .

1986 There were no 100-loss turkeys. Gobble, gobble.

1987 Julio Franco *(Cleveland Indians 61–101).* Back in the 1980s, Cleveland was one of the sorriest franchises in baseball. Since we just finished a rundown on another inept Indians team (1985), we're going to keep this one short. Notwithstanding their 101 losses, the Tribe did have a few guys who deserved an INBB. With a .319 AVG, .389 OBP, and 33 steals, Franco was one of their "chosen few."

1987 Other Guys Who Done Good Despite the 101 Losses and Merit INBBs *(Cleveland Indians).*

- Joe Carter, who hit 32 home runs, knocked in 106 and stole 31 bases.
- Brook Jacoby homered 32 times to go along with a .300 AVG and .387 OBP.
- Cory Snyder beat Carter and Jacoby in the HR department with his 33 round-trippers. The Indians' right fielder also compiled 82 RBI.
- Designated Hitter Pat Tabler plated 86 teammates on his way to a final .307 AVG.
- Lead-off man Brett Butler had another outstanding season in 1987 (.295 AVG, .399 OBP, 33 steals) to cop his second INBB Award.

Once again, as in 1985, the Tribe's problem in 1987 was not their offense. Their pitching staff reeked with their "ace" Tom Candiotti, who went 7–18 and registered a whopping 4.78 ERA. The only bright spot was reliever Doug Jones who went 6–5 with a good 3.15 ERA. The rest of the guys in the bullpen had ERA figures ranging from 4.65 to 5.67. Doug Jones snagged an INBB Award for his efforts.

1988 Eddie Murray *(Baltimore Orioles 54–107)*. The once-proud O's collapsed in 1988 but don't blame any of that lost season on Eddie Murray. "Steady" Eddie blasted 28 home runs to go along with a .284 average and .361 OBP.

1988 Cal Ripken, Jr. *(Baltimore Orioles)*. It wasn't Junior's fault, either. His line: .264 AVG, .372 OBP, 23 HR, 81 RBI. It was typical Ripken-at-his-peak production during a very un-Oriole-like season.

Junior was undeniably one of the greatest shortstops in baseball history, and I don't want to denigrate his legacy, but since retirement, with that bald head of his, doesn't he resemble Uncle Fester from the *Addams Family*? I mean, stick a lightbulb in his mouth, and it's move over Jackie Coogan and Christopher Lloyd!

1988 Joe Orsulak *(Baltimore Orioles)*. Joseph Michael earned an *additional* INBB with a first-rate .288 average and decent .331 OBP. Together, the Orioles registered a batting mark of .238 and OBP of .305, both of which ranked last in the American League. Baltimore also finished 14th out of 14 teams in hits, runs, and slugging.

1988 Gerald Perry *(Atlanta Braves 54–106)*. Perry's efforts in Atlanta's ill-fated 1988 season earned him his only berth on the NL All-Star team. The left-handed swinging Perry batted .300, drove in 74 runs, and stole 29 bases. He was one of two Braves to cop an INBB Award for their team's dreadful campaign. However, two of his teammates deserved Honorable Mentions:

- Second baseman Ron Gant (24 HR, 8 triples, 60 RBI in 1988). A poor .317 OBP and 118 K were deciding factors in denying Mr. Gant the top award. He was also brutal in the field, leading the league in errors at second. A rookie in 1988, Gant would eventually be moved to the outfield, where he would thrive and become a top-notch player.
- Dale Murphy was on the backside of his productive career in 1988 and only hit .226 and fanned 125 times. But he did crash 24 home

runs, 35 doubles, and knocked in 77 Braves. Had that average and OBP (.313) been a lot higher, the former first-round pick would have snared an INBB outright instead of an honorable mention.

Two hurlers on the 1988 Braves gave Atlanta fans occasional glimpses of what good major league pitching looks like. For their efforts on the mound, these two hurlers have earned an INBB Award:

- Jose Alvarez (2.99 ERA, 88 hits allowed and 81 K in 102 innings)
- Paul Assenmacher (3.06 ERA, 72 hits allowed and 71 K in 79 innings)

Sort of Random Trivia: In need of a catcher, the 1962 Mets acquired Harry Chiti from the Indians for a player to be named later. After 43 plate appearances and a .195 BA, the Mets figured they already had enough underperformers (on a team that would eventually lose 120 games) and sent Chiti back to the Tribe as that player to be named later.

1989 Lou Whitaker *(Detroit Tigers, 59–103)*. A holdover from the 1984 Detroit juggernaut that captured the AL pennant and World Championship, Whitaker kept on producing despite the 1988 club's profound lack of success. The seasoned second sacker's batting average (.251) was unremarkable, but among his 128 hits were 28 home runs and 21 doubles. His OBP was a valuable .361, and he drove in 85 runs.

1989 Gary Pettis *(Detroit Tigers)*. Speedster Pettis walked 84 times, a figure which contributed heavily to an excellent .375 OBP. Whenever the man got on base, he was a threat to go and swiped 43 bases (fourth-best in the league). A nothing special .257 batting average is countered with a fourth Gold Glove Award for his work in the outfield.

1989 Mike Henneman *(Detroit Tigers)*. The tall right-handed reliever was the only pitcher on the 1989 Tiger staff with a winning record (11–4). He allowed only 4 home runs over his 60 appearances while compiling an OK 3.70 ERA.

1989 Frank Tanana *(Detroit Tigers)*. Skipper Sparky Anderson's ace, Tanana, went 10–14 with a 3.58 ERA. He struck out 147 in 223 innings pitched, hurled 6 complete games, and finished the season with an adequate

1.346 WHIP. The rest of Detroit's rotation went a combined 20–43. The starter with the next lowest ERA was Kevin Ritz, with a bloated 4.38.

That's it. The INBB selections for the decade of the 1980s are complete. I must admit, I do feel a little guilty about my quip about Cal Ripken, Jr. He's a good man and has done a lot for the community he lives in. If you're a die-hard Oriole/or Ripken fan, I apologize. I probably should have never mentioned the fact that I think he looks like Uncle Fester.

My mother once told me that some things are better left unsaid.

I hope you can find it in your heart to forgive me.

Brett Butler was a fine player on some very bad teams. (Courtesy Arturo Pardavila III/Creative Commons)

Mike Krukow's resume for 1985 includes a 3.38 ERA and 1.156 WHIP. (tradingcarddb.com)

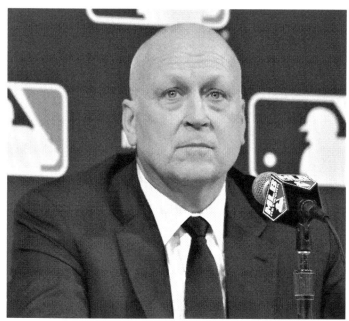

Cal Ripken, Jr. The Committee thinks a bald head looks much better than a bad rug. (Courtesy Arturo Pardavila III/Creative Commons)

Give that man an Orioles cap!

Mobile phones began to appear on the market in the 1980s. By the 21st century, fans were able to watch their favorite team play on their device.

Pitching for a club that lost 104 games didn't keep Cecilio Guante from posting outstanding numbers. (tradingcarddb.com)

The relief pitching heroics of Tug McGraw propelled the Phillies to the 1980 World Championship.

The 1990s

Read My Lips

Some important stuff that happened in the 1990s:

- The Hubble Space Telescope was launched during a U.S. Space Shuttle mission on April 24, 1990. It is one of the largest satellites ever to be placed in orbit. A major breakthrough in astrophysics, Hubble offered a much deeper view into space.

- In 1990, the World Wide Web debuted as an electronic information system. Within a few years, almost every area of life in the developed world are profoundly impacted.

- Led by the United States, a coalition of 35 nations drove Iraqi armed forces out of Kuwait in just 100 hours. "Operation Desert Storm" ended on February 28, 1991.

- Hurricane Andrew ripped through southern Florida and south-central Louisiana in August 1992. The category five storm claims 65 lives and causes 26 billion in damages.

- On January 20, 1993, William Jefferson Clinton became the first "Baby Boomer" to ascend to the Presidency of the United States. A "Boomer" was a baby born in the U.S. during the post-World War II period of 1946-1964.

- Terrorists attempted to topple the twin towers of the World Trade Center by exploding a truck bomb in the center's underground parking garage. Six people were killed and 1,000 injured in the February 26, 1993 attack.

- A 6.7 magnitude earthquake, the epicenter located 20 miles northwest of Los Angeles, killed 72 and injured 9,000 on January 17, 1994.

Nicknamed for the community near the epicenter, "The Northridge Earthquake" resulted in an estimated 20-50 billion dollars damage.

- At least a third of the Murrah Federal Building in Oklahoma City was blasted away by a powerful truck bomb. Domestic terrorists are blamed; 168 lose their lives, and 800 are wounded.

- With Chief Justice William Rehnquist presiding, The U.S. Senate voted to exonerate President Clinton of perjury charges and obstruction of justice. The 21-day trial ended on February 12, 1999.

- On March 12, 1999, the Dow Jones Industrial Average hit the 10,000 mark for the first time in its 114-year history.

Some important stuff that happened in Major League Baseball in the 1990s:

- 43-year-old Nolan Ryan threw his 6th career no-hitter on June 11, 1990. The Texas Rangers hurler would toss yet another "no-no" in 1991.

- Speedster Ricky Henderson swiped the 938th base of his career, eclipsing Lou Brock's stolen base record. May 1991.

- By the middle of the 1990s, over 200 major league players were making salaries of over one million dollars a year.

- The 1994 season ended 52 games early as the Major League Players Association went on strike. Because of the work stoppage, there were no playoffs or World Series in the Fall. A settlement was eventually reached, and play finally resumed 18 games into the 1995 campaign.

- Future Hall of Famers Ozzie Smith, Dave Winfield, Kirby Puckett, and Andre Dawson retired in 1996.

- Regular season play between American and National League teams debuted when the Texas Rangers hosted the San Francisco Giants in Arlington on June 12, 1997.

- Major League Baseball expanded by adding two teams for the 1998 season. The new entries are the Tampa Bay Devil Rays in the American League and the Arizona Diamondbacks in the National League.

- In 1998, Mark McGuire of the Cardinals and the Cubs' Sammy Sosa made successful assaults on Babe Ruth's single-season record of 60 home runs. McGuire finishes with 70 and Sosa with 66, but later revelations of steroid use by the pair darken their accomplishments.

- Believing their collective bargaining agreement had been violated, 57 major league umpires threatened to resign on September 1, 1999, if their demands are unmet. Major League Baseball accepted 22 of the resignations and replaced them with minor league umpires. In disarray, the union (MULA) was decertified and is replaced by the World Umpires Association (WUA).

◆ ◆ ◆

The decade got off to a good (?) start in **1990,** with no one sinking to the depths of a 100-loss season. But it wouldn't be long before the Committee had an ample supply of players on epically rotten teams to honor yadda, yadda, yadda . . .

The envelopes, please.

1991 Carlos Baerga *(Cleveland Indians 57-105)*. He led AL second basemen in errors with 27 but the 2nd year player did all right with the stick (.288 BA, .346 OBP, 11 HR, 69 RBI, 80 runs). Indians fans loved the fact that he worked hard and hustled. Many were quite upset when the Tribe traded him to the Mets in 1996.

1991 Albert Belle *(Cleveland Indians)*. The photo for Belle's page at www.baseballreference.com (one of the best stats sites on the 'net) shows Sir Albert smiling. It must have been taken at a bad angle or something. Maybe a sportswriter had just slipped and fallen. There has to be an explanation . . .

Legendary for being a nasty dude, Belle put up some mean numbers (28 HR, 95 RBI, .540 SLG).

1991 Alex Cole *(Cleveland Indians)*. A speedy outfielder who stole 27 bases in 122 games. Good batting average (.295) and on-base percentage, too (.386).

1991 Greg Swindell and pals *(Cleveland Indians)*. The Tribe's pitching staff wasn't hopeless in 1991, allowing the least number of walks in the league and the second-lowest number of home runs surrendered. Less impressive but still notable were 9th place finishes out of 14 teams in ERA and earned runs. Swindell was a big reason for the staff's flirtation with respectability (3.48 ERA, 1.143 WHIP, 169 K, and just 43 walks over 238 innings pitched).

Also aiding in the Indians' cause and securing INBBs were:

- Rod Nichols (3.54 ERA, 1.274 WHIP)
- Tom Candiotti (2.24 ERA, 1.071 WHIP)
- Jeff Shaw (3.36 ERA, 1.369 WHIP)
- Steve Olin. The case for the team's closer was a tough one to decide. The 410th pick in the 1987 Amateur Draft did save 17 games to go along with a nice 3.36 ERA. But his hits-per-innings pitched ratio was a little troubling (1.491). The saves and ERA stats carry his season across the INBB finish line.

Cleveland starter Charles Nagy qualifies for an Honorable mention for recording 10 wins and a 1.391 WHIP.

Why no INBB?

A high 4.13 ERA kept him from reaching that lofty height.

1992 Major League Baseball saw no team sink to the depths of one-hundred losses. The Dodgers barely escaped such infamy by dropping 99.

1993 Eddie Murray *(New York Mets 59-103)*. One more INBB for Murray, this one for a stellar performance in a Metropolitans uniform (Did you know that the team nickname "Mets" is a shortened version of the club's full name of "Metropolitans"? I did and thought you might find it mildly interesting if not downright revelatory). The 37-year-old future Hall of Famer hit .285, drilled 28 homers, and drove in 100 runs.

1993 Jeff Kent *(New York Mets)*. .270 AVG + 21 HR + 80 RBI = INBB Award.

1993 Bobby Bonilla *(New York Mets)*. After underperforming the year before and enduring the caustic criticism of Mets fans and the media, Bonilla rebounded in 1993. He contributed 34 HR, 87 RBI, and got on base at a .352 clip, but the Mets still finished in last. They couldn't blame "Bobby Bo" for *that* one.

1993 Todd Hundley *(New York Mets)*. He is the son of former Major League catcher Randy Hundley. (I guess many of you already knew that). Unlike his daddy, Todd was no wiz behind the plate, and it was relatively easy to steal on him. His batting average (.228) and on-base percentage were awful, BUT he did make the most of his 95 hits by hitting 11 home runs and driving in 53. Randy's boy gets an Honorable Mention by making up for a lot of his defensive deficiencies by producing runs at a fair clip for the Mets' offense.

1993 Joe Orsulak *(New York Mets)*. Where have we heard that name before? Joe was a steady, dependable player over a 14-year career. He played all three outfield positions plus put in few innings at first base for the Mets in 1993. As a batter, he hit a worthy .284 with a satisfactory .331 OBP. He was mainly a singles hitter (albeit a good one) and a more than adequate fielder. Had he delivered a little more power (only 27 extra-base hits in 449 plate appearances), the Committee might have presented him with another INBB. He gets an Honorable Mention instead, which isn't so bad.

1993 Dwight Gooden *(New York Mets)*. In between stints in rehab for cocaine abuse, Gooden was straight enough to put in a good season (12 wins, 3.45 ERA, 1.193 WHIP, 149 K in 209 innings pitched). Some of his teammates pitched well, too, and earned INBBs. The Mets' problem was that these bright spots didn't pitch enough innings collectively to help the club climb out of the basement. They are:

Brett Saberhagen (3.29 ERA, 1.062 WHIP, 139 innings pitched).
Sid Fernandez (2.93 ERA, 0.986 WHIP, 120 innings pitched).
Mike Maddox (3.60 ERA, 1.253 WHIP, 75 innings pitched).
Bobby Jones (3.65 ERA, 1.346 WHIP, 62 innings pitched).

By comparison, five of the other gentlemen on the staff who were used the most had ERAs ranging from 4.11 to 5.20.

1993 Tony Gwynn *(San Diego Padres 61-101)*. A hit machine (.358 BA, .398 OBP) also led his team in stolen bases with 14. Nicknamed "Mr. Padre," Gwynn was humble about his accomplishments:
"I am a natural hitter, but I have to work hard to keep it," he said.

Gwynn must have worked *very* hard; over the next four seasons, he compiled batting averages of .394, .368, .353, and .372.

1993 Phil Plantier *(San Diego Padres)*. It was a career year for the Padres' left-fielder. He smacked 34 home runs and drove in 100. Also, a .980 fielding percentage and 14 assists placed him 2nd in the league in both categories.

1993 Derek Bell *(San Diego Padres)*. Twenty-one HR and 72 RBI compensated for a weak .303 OBP. Those twenty-six stolen bases helped, too.

1993 Andy Benes *(San Diego Padres)*. One of the best fielding pitchers in the league, the ace of the Padres' staff, won 15 games, recorded a 3.78 ERA, 1.240 WHIP, and whiffed 178 batters over 231 innings. It was an All-Star (and INBB) caliber season for Benes.

1993 Greg Harris *(San Diego Padres)*. The ship was on its' way down to the bottom of the NL West, but Harris managed to keep his "head above water" (another one of those cliches-this would not be a *real* baseball book without a few well-worn chestnuts). He was the only one on the staff who pitched more than fifty innings to put up a winning record (10-9), and his 3.67 ERA was the lowest of the Padres' rotation. The "icing on the cake" (cliché city, again) is a fine 1.250 WHIP. Two thumbs-up and a virtual pat on the back for the Greensboro, North Carolina native!

1993 Wally Whitehurst *(San Diego Padres)*. OK season performance from a non-spectacular seven-year major league career. Noteworthy because Whitehurst's 3.83 ERA and 1.315 WHIP were better numbers than those compiled by many of his mound mates.

1993 Gene Harris *(San Diego Padres)*. This was another toughie. Harris did save 23 games, and his ERA was first-rate (3.03). However, his WHIP was poor (1.584), thanks largely to issuing 37 walks in 59 innings. Should the team's closer be awarded an INBB, or was his performance the stuff Honorable Mentions are made of?

The Committee has come to a resolution regarding this matter. They have decided to allow you, the highly knowledgeable baseball fan, to decide. Just use the blank line below:

With a #2 Pencil or pen with black or blue ink or crayon, write your choice "INBB" or "Honorable Mention."

1994 A large chunk of the season was lost due to another strike by the players. One of the ramifications of this unfortunate development were no 100-loss teams to regale . . .

AND

. . . this same strike extended into a portion of the **1995** schedule. Fewer games played almost assuredly prevented any teams from reverse scaling the depths of a 100-loss season.

1996 Travis Fryman *(Detroit Tigers 53-109)*. A major "hole" in his game was a tendency to strike out a lot; Fryman averaged 131 whiffs per 162 games played during his career. Besides that, he was a good player. 1996 was one of his best at the plate (22 HR, 100 RBI). With the glove, Fryman had the highest fielding percentage of any third basemen in the AL (.979) and was #1 at the position in assists (126).

1996 Bobby Higginson *(Detroit Tigers)*. Drafted by the Tigers in 1992, the Philadelphia native and Temple University alum played his entire 11-year career with Detroit. The hometown Phillies had drafted him the year before, but Higginson passed on the opportunity to wear the red pinstripes (I don't know exactly how that fits into the discussion about Higginson's INBB worthiness, but I thought you might appreciate that tidbit of information).

In his 2nd year, the outfielder blossomed with a .320 AVG, .404 OBP, 26 HR, 81 RBI, and scored 75 runs. Not bad totals on a team that finished last in batting average (.256) and on-base percentage (.323), along with leading the league in strikeouts (1268).

Three other Tigers merited INBB recognition:

- First baseman Cecil Fielder (26 HR, 80 RBI)
- Outfielder Melvin Nieves (24 HR, 60 RBI)
- Second baseman Mark Lewis (11 HR, 55 RBI)

Fielder and Lewis fielded their positions well, Nieves not so skillfully.

No one on Detroit's pitching staff came close to earning either an INBB or Honorable Mention. The staff ERA was a whopping 6.38, the WHIP an embarrassing 1.733, and, ah, heck, you get the idea. They wuz *bad*.

1997 "One-hundred loss seasons, there were no." —Yoda

1998 Derek Lee *(Florida Marlins 54-108)*. Marlin's fans witnessed one of the fastest franchise collapses in baseball history. World Champs in 1997, financial pressures forced ownership to jettison the stars on the roster that were making big bucks. The result was a complete reversal of fortune, with the team freefalling to the NL East basement and 108 losses. However, there were glimmers of quality play that softened the pain for fans who watched a wretched team.

First baseman Derek Lee showed the potential that would eventually result in 331 career home runs over a 15-year career. The batting average (.233) and OBP (.318) in 1998 were sub-par, but 17 HR and 74 RBI made pitchers notice. The 22-year-old rookie was also real slick with the glove, logging an excellent .993 fielding percentage.

1998 Craig Counsel *(Florida Marlins)*. Another youngster given a chance to shine following Florida's purge of high-price vets. Counsel's light would blaze brighter as the years progressed. He got off to a satisfactory start with a .251 BA and .355 OBP, and as a second baseman, he was sure-handed, committing only five errors for a .991 fielding percentage.

1998 Edgar Renteria *(Florida Marlins)*. A beloved figure in his homeland of Columbia, Renteria was on his way to establishing himself as one of the best shortstops in the Majors when he hit .282, stole 41 bases, and scored 79 runs. Renteria would play another 13 years, hitting as high as .330 and driving in as many as 100 runs, and be named to five All-Star teams. As impressive as his resume is, perhaps someday his greatest claim-to-fame will be the prestigious and much-coveted "I Am Not A Baseball Bozo" Award he secured for his work in 1998.

1998 Cliff Floyd *(Florida Marlins)*. The big man (6'5", 220 pounds) rocked NL hurlers for 22 home runs, 90 RBI, and scored 85 runs. Not a ponderous giant, the left fielder stole 27 bases to lead the Marlins.

Sort of Random Trivia: Did you know that the Marlins were the first and (as of 2021) the only team to win the World Championship one year and then finish dead last the next? Do you care?

1998 Mark Kotsay *(Florida Marlins)*. The .318 OBP didn't exactly "wow" anyone, but the rest of his line was pretty good (.279 AVG, 11 HR, 68 RBI, 77 runs, 10 steals). Stationed in rightfield, the 22-year-old Kotsay recorded 15 assists.

1999 Let's party like it's 1999! Yeah, yeah. No 100-loss teams!

Wow. We're done. The Committee and I would like to thank you for hanging in there with us. To show how much they appreciated your participation, the Committee has voted unanimously to confer you with an honorary "I Am Not a Baseball Bozo" Award of your own! Isn't that thrilling? You certainly deserved an INBB after giving rapt attention to the preceding pages (not to mention having tolerated the dumb humor and corny ad-libs sprinkled throughout).

It's two thumbs-up and a hearty virtual pat on the back for you!

21 dingers in 1993 for infielder Jeff Kent. (Courtesy
Ryosuke Yag/Creative Commons)

Dwight Gooden fought through
a battle with cocaine addiction to
win 12 games in 1993. (Courtesy
Barry Colla Photography)

As a sort-of-regular player in 1996, Cecil
Fielder hit 26 HR and knocked-in 80.
(Courtesy Creative Commons)

Nolan Ryan was a mere 43 years old when he tossed his
7th no-hitter in 1991. (Courtesy Chuck Anderson/Creative
Commons)

Portions of Florida and Louisiana were devasted by Hurricane Andrew in August
1992. (Courtesy U.S. National Oceanic and Atmospheric Administration)

A microscopic 0.986 in 1993 helped Sid Fernandez win an INBB. (Courtesy Jeff Marquis/Creative Commons)

The U.S. and dozens of other nations militarily drive Iraqi forces out of Kuwait in February 1991.

This picture of Hall-of-Famer Joe DiMaggio and some pretty girl he knew was thrown-in here just for the heck of it.

In 1998, the Marlins gave second baseman Craig Counsell a chance to be a starter. (Courtesy Creative Commons)

Bibliography

BOOKS

Cohen, Richard and Neft, David, *The Sports Encyclopedia Baseball: 2004*, (St. Martins Griffin, New York, NY, 2004)

James, Bill, *The New Bill James Historical Abstract*, (New York, NY: Free Press, 2003)

Prebenna, David, *The Baseball Encyclopedia,* (New York, NY: Simon and Shuster, 1996)

Ritter, Lawrence S., *The Glory of Their Times*, (New York, NY: Harper Perennial Modern Classics, 2010 edition

Kashatus, Williams C., *Dick Allen: The Life and Times of a Baseball Immortal*, (Atglen, PA; Schiffler Publishing, Ltd., 2017)

Macht, Norman L., *The Grand Old Man of Baseball Connie Mack: His Final Years*, 1932-1956, (Lincoln and London; University of Nebraska Press 2015)

White, Bill, *Uppity: My Untold Story About the Games People Play*, (New York, NY, Grand Central Publishing, 2011)

Donley, Brendan, *The 1968 World Series: The Tigers-Cardinals Classic as Told by the Men Who Played*, (New York, NY, Sports Publishing, 2018, 2020)

WEBSITES

Baseball Timeline | PBS

1930s Baseball: History, MVPs & MLB Champions (retrowaste.com)

Baseball History in the 1930s: Dog Days of the Depression (thisgreatgame.com)

https://www.thoughtco.com/1950s-timeline-1779952

Elvis Presley's First Recording Session | HowStuffWorks

50 years on, the Dick Allen-Frank Thomas fight still resonates (inquirer.com) article by Frank Fitzpatrick July 2, 2015.

1940s Timeline (softschools.com)

1960s Timeline (softschools.com)

The 1970s Timeline (softschools.com)

1970 – 1979 World History (infoplease.com)

Best Baseball Quotes of All Time – Motivating and Funny Quotes (menshealth.com)

Jeff Burroughs – Society for American Baseball Research (sabr.org)

Nate Colbert – Society for American Baseball Research (sabr.org)

Eddie Rommel – Society for American Baseball Research (sabr.org)

Dave Keefe – Society for American Baseball Research (sabr.org)

Frank Welch – Society for American Baseball Research (sabr.org)

Stuffy McInnis – Society for American Baseball Research (sabr.org)

Doc Prothro – Society for American Baseball Research (sabr.org)

Ira Flagstead – Society for American Baseball Research (sabr.org)
Fresco Thompson – Society for American Baseball Research (sabr.org)
Clarence Mitchell – Society for American Baseball Research (sabr.org)
Billy Meyer – Society for American Baseball Research (sabr.org)
Jack Russell – Society for American Baseball Research (sabr.org)
Earl Webb – Society for American Baseball Research (sabr.org)
Smead Jolley – Society for American Baseball Research (sabr.org)
Ed Durham – Society for American Baseball Research (sabr.org)
Bob Johnson – Society for American Baseball Research (sabr.org)
George Puccinelli – Society for American Baseball Research (sabr.org)
Sam West – Society for American Baseball Research (sabr.org)
Morrie Arnovich – Society for American Baseball Research (sabr.org)
Wally Moses – Society for American Baseball Research (sabr.org)
Kirby Higbe – Society for American Baseball Research (sabr.org)
Jo-Jo White – Society for American Baseball Research (sabr.org)
Jesse Flores – Society for American Baseball Research (sabr.org)
Phil Marchildon – Society for American Baseball Research (sabr.org)
Dave Philley – Society for American Baseball Research (sabr.org)
Al Evans – Society for American Baseball Research (sabr.org)
Jeffrey Leonard – Society for American Baseball Research (sabr.org)
Satchel Paige – Society for American Baseball Research (sabr.org)
Carlos Baerga – Society for American Baseball Research (sabr.org)
Bobby Bonilla – Society for American Baseball Research (sabr.org)
Dwight Gooden – Society for American Baseball Research (sabr.org)
Tony Gwynn – Society for American Baseball Research (sabr.org)
All-American Girls Professional Baseball League | History & Facts | Britannica
Timeline – 1940s | Philadelphia Phillies (mlb.com)
1980s' Timeline: Important Events of the '80s Everyone Should Know – Historyplex
1980s Sports: History, Facts, MVPs & Champions (retrowaste.com)
baseball.fandom.com/wiki/1981_baseball_strike
Baseball Events in History – BrainyHistory
Eruption History of Mount St. Helens through start of Holocene (usgs.gov)
Tiananmen Square incident | Summary, Details, & Facts | Britannica
Fall of the Berlin Wall and Reunification (1989–1990) | Culture| Arts, music and lifestyle reporting from Germany | DW | 22.04.2013
Ueberroth Suspends Seven Players for Use of Drugs – Los Angeles Times (latimes.com)
Jim Thorpe Gets His Medals 70 Years After They Were Taken Away January 18, 1983 (sportshistorytoday.com)
What if the Phillies had been able to avoid the 1964 collapse by making a trade seven years earlier? (inquirer.com)
Timeline: 2000-2009 – I Love the 2000s (weebly.com)
World Events From 2000-2009 timeline | Timetoast timelines
A Timeline of Baseball – History and Headlines
Major League Baseball Players by Year of Death (baseball-almanac.com)

General History | MiLB.com
Weird Baseball Facts and Trivia (thehypertexts.com)
35 Odd Baseball Facts That Are Too Strange To Be Made Up (buzzfeed.com)
Baseball Almanac – Baseball Anecdotes & Stories (baseball-almanac.com)
95 Baseball Facts, Trivia, and More | FactRetriever.com
Dock Ellis' bizarre no-hitter while on LSD: 50 years later (nypost.com)
Baseball Top 50 Funny Quotes About Baseball (aarp.org)
Koufax and Drysdale held out 53 years ago | by Dan Lovallo | Medium

About the Author

Chris Williams is a freelance writer with numerous short stories and feature articles to his credit. In addition, he has had two volumes of historical baseball essays published, including *Stealing First and Other Old-Time Baseball Stories* (Sunbury Press 2020) Also, he has a series of children's books about working dogs to his credit and a religious book about biblical Eschatology.

When not hunched over a keyboard working on a writing project, Chris works as a certified Level 3 Dog Trainer at a large chain pet store in Hanover, PA.

He and his wife Sue have lived in York County, Pennsylvania since 1990. Learn more at AuthorChrisWilliams.com.

Made in the USA
Middletown, DE
09 October 2021